Your Towns and Cities in

Rotherham
in the Great War

Your Towns and Cities in the Great War

Rotherham
in the Great War

Margaret Drinkall

Pen & Sword
MILITARY

First published in Great Britain in 2014 by
PEN & SWORD MILITARY
An imprint of
Pen & Sword Books Ltd
47 Church Street
Barnsley
South Yorkshire, S70 2AS

Copyright © Margaret Drinkall, 2014

ISBN 978 1 78383 149 4

Printed and bound in England by
CPI Group (UK) Ltd, Croydon, CR0 4YY

Pen & Sword Books Ltd incorporates the imprints of Aviation, Atlas,
Family History, Fiction, Maritime, Military, Discovery, Politics, History,
Archaeology, Select, Wharncliffe Local History, Wharncliffe True Crime,
Military Classics, Wharncliffe Transport, Leo Cooper, The Praetorian
Press, Remember When, Seaforth Publishing and Frontline Publishing.

For a complete list of Pen & Sword titles please contact
PEN & SWORD BOOKS LIMITED
47 Church Street, Barnsley, South Yorkshire, S70 2AS, England
E-mail: enquiries@pen-and-sword.co.uk
Website: www.pen-and-sword.co.uk

Contents

Foreword by Sarah Champion MP for Rotherham   6

Acknowledgements   9

Introduction   11

1   War clouds gather   15

2   The realities of warfare   29

3   Life in the trenches   41

4   Impact on family life   55

5   Anti-German feeling in Rotherham   71

6   Modern technology   83

7   The RAMC and wounded soldiers   97

8   The Rotherham police force   107

9   The end of the war   119

Bibliography and Further Reading   133

Index   135

Foreword

Local author Margaret Drinkall is renowned for her previous works on history in and around Rotherham and has now written a book that chronicles what life was like in the town during the years of the Great War, for which I am honoured and delighted to be writing the foreword.

Modern historians recognise that first-hand accounts of the period are rapidly diminishing and it is important to ensure that these history-shaping moments in time are never forgotten. Margaret's methodical research utilising newspapers, archive material, local council minutes and military accounts has managed to reveal a side of the town that will resonate with modern-day Rotherham.

The book examines the massive recruitment drives that resulted in over 29,000 Rotherham and district men enlisting during the years between 1914 – 1918 and the stories behind the news of the war. The book highlights the incredible courage shown, using text from letters from men informing relatives of their lives in the trenches and suffering the horrors of mud, disease and gas attacks.

It is a matter of fact that war tears families apart and the accounts of the devastation wrought on local people hearing news of the death of a beloved son or brother are simply harrowing to read, but perhaps the saddest part is reading of the frequent requests in local newspapers for information on missing relatives whose remains were never found. The author draws heavily on personal accounts, such as the Rotherham man who survived the sinking of the *Lusitania*, courageous deeds on the front line and experiences of men wounded in battle, unable to move for fear of German snipers.

Yet, throughout the book, the fortitude of Rotherham men, many from farms and collieries around the town who had previously never even held let alone fired a gun, stands out. After the excitement of enlistment and the most basic of training, they were thrust into battle and faced death on a daily basis. These were the true heroes of the Great War. Ordinary people from the town were now stretcher-bearers, going out night after night into No-Man's-Land to look for their wounded comrades, with women serving with the Royal Army Medical Corps treating soldiers, both British and German, in makeshift first-aid posts of converted cattle sheds and schools.

Perhaps, though, the most poignant part of the book comes from the personal accounts of surviving relatives. Here Margaret really does manage to bring to life letters from the Front, many written by those who did not survive. For those who did, of course, the truth is that the real pain and suffering survived long after the last bullet was fired. Soldiers wrote letters to loved ones full of yearning to simply be back home with their families. Almost all revealed a wish to return to Rotherham and many hoped the war would soon be over.

Many who did return never spoke about their time on the front line, although some had photograph albums showing comrades they shared experiences with. The majority just wanted to get on with their lives, to get back to the normality they had before the war. Others were so emotionally damaged by the experience of battle they became known as war-broken men. Cases that we now refer to as shell-shock were recognised in the early years of the war by forward-thinking Rotherham workhouse officials who lobbied the government to have these men treated in specialist hospitals, instead of the workhouse lunatic wards that were very much the norm.

Even though these accounts are a century old, what is obvious is that they still echo the feelings of families of soldiers involved in modern warfare today. The need to remember the past involves people naming children after places where soldiers fell, accounts of women losing sons and going grey overnight while others cling onto an identity bracelet of a beloved son who will never return. There is no doubt that the men and woman of Rotherham showed immense courage and fortitude during the years of the Great War and relatives that still live in Rotherham today remember and honour their dead, not just on Remembrance Day but on ordinary days all through the year.

It is incredibly important to remember those who have fought for their country in the past, and in doing this remember those who continue to do so. It is hoped that their stories continue to be told to younger generations through wonderful books such as this one to ensure they will never be forgotten.

Sarah Champion MP
Member of Parliament for Rotherham
January 2014

Acknowledgements

I am incredibly thankful for the research undertaken by Jayne Daley, Andy Featherstone and Les Gilberthorpe, which is available at the Rotherham Archives and Local Studies based at Clifton Park. Jayne and Andy have indexed material on various military related projects, including the Rotherham and District Honours and Awards Index for World War One. Further indexing for World War Two will shortly be available for use. Andy Featherstone and Frank Westwood have produced a book listing all the names on the various war memorials in the Rotherham area. Andy, Jayne and Les have used information available in the two local newspapers, the *Rotherham Advertiser* and the *South Yorkshire Times* (Mexborough and Swinton edition). It is hoped that their work will enable family history researchers to locate articles and photos on recipients of the Military Medal, Distinguished Conduct Medal, etc. The results of their research are available at the Archives, so anyone who is interested in finding out more about relatives, please speak to a member of staff, who will be able to help.

Also I have to thank: Ann Mapplebeck for sharing her memories of her great-uncles, Sidney James, John Henry and Joseph Arthur Beverley; Christopher Page and family for their memories and memorabilia of their relatives John William Page, Francis Page and John Hersin Page; Sandra Housley for permission to read and reproduce the letters of Samuel Maiden; Sue Duty for the information on the Porter family; and perhaps most of all for permission to include some of the World War One memorabilia belonging to the private collection of Kathleen and Neil Senior and for the memories of her father and grandfather, Frederick Abel and Harry Abel.

I am very grateful to Rotherham MP Sarah Champion for taking the time out of her busy schedule to write the foreward to the book and also to her PA, Vanessa Johns, for her help. Writing any book is always a team effort and I could not have achieved this without the help of Pen and Sword Publishing and the skilful editing of Diane Parkin. I would also like to thank the staff at the Rotherham Archives and Local Studies, as always for their unfailing help.

Last but by no means least I would like to thank my son Chris for his help with the illustrations and his skilful knowledge on enhancing the pictures.

Margaret Drinkall
Rotherham
January 2014

Introduction

The aim of this book is to illustrate what impact the Great War had on the town of Rotherham, South Yorkshire. Included are some of the stories of the very patriotic men who enlisted in their thousands to serve king and country. Men who had no experience of warfare unhesitatingly left their jobs to fight in a war. For some of these men it would be the first time they had travelled beyond the neighbouring towns of Sheffield and Doncaster, while many others would never see the town of their birth again.

Memories of the Great War are fading fast for most people and the only thing that many families have to remind them of that time are the artefacts and medals of relatives lost in battle. All soldiers who fought in the Great War received a War Medal, and for some that is all that remains of sons, brothers and father. Only at the end of the war was the cost of the scale of violence and destruction truly counted. The former world that the men and women of Rotherham had formerly known had been changed forever.

In this book I wanted to look not only at the brave men who fought on the front line but also the men and women who put up with the problems experienced in warfare. Areas I have not covered (i.e. munitions, spies and accusations of shirkers in the town) have been covered elsewhere. In my research for the book, I found many heroes but I also found stories about real people who might be termed as rogues and rascals of the time. Men such as Samuel Maiden who went AWOL from the army in 1912 when his wife gave birth to a little daughter called Rosie. Aware that the military authorities might still be looking for him, this did not stop him from enlisting under another name when war broke out. During his enforced separation from his wife and new daughter he wrote several poignant letters home.

I also found details of two brothers called Beverley, the youngest of whom enlisted at 16. Undoubtedly courageous, nevertheless he rebelled against the military authorities and the need for mindless obedience that they tried to inculcate in the soldiers. His conduct sheet reveals the charges against him, which were mostly returning late back to his regiment after leave. His older brother was more reserved and served his time with only one tiny transgression.

All three men ended up dying for their country in a foreign land. Research also uncovered the story of Sydney James, a professional footballer for Huddersfield Town, who enlisted and died after being given a white feather for cowardice.

The Great War Medal

This is also the story of a town during the Great War where giddy girls were reported to be throwing themselves at men in khaki. The situation became so intolerable, that a committee was formed to look into the morals of the young people of Rotherham. Another revelation, which incensed the whole country, was the Clifton Park Scandal, which was reported in the national newspapers. As a result it was said that the people of Rotherham 'should hang their heads in shame and disgust'. The town also saw disgraceful anti-German riots that shook the authorities to its core, as looters were chased by mounted police through thoroughfares that are so familiar to us today. At that time German people who had lived peacefully were looked on with suspicion from former friends and neighbours. Those who tried to enlist were mostly turned away as spies. One Rotherham man who did manage to enlist, spent most of the war in a German prisoner-of-war camp.

Harry Able, was a respectable man who had a strong

The War Memorial in Clifton Park, Rotherham

sense of justice. This belief was shattered when after the war he returned home and heard about the treatment suffered by his wife and children in his absence. Others who also thankfully returned back to the town were the three Porter brothers. Rotherham was also the place where zeppelins instead of arousing fear just generated curiosity. The

The Memorial Rock Garden in Clifton Park, Rotherham

police and military authorities issued firm instructions on where people of Rotherham were to go in the event of an air raid, but the population came out in their hundreds to see the huge lumbering airships that dropped bombs in their midst.

Although memories of the Great War fade, the town still remembers the brave soldiers, whose names are inscribed on the War Memorial in Clifton Park. There is also a Garden of Remembrance, which lists the names of Rotherham men awarded the VC, and a Memorial rock garden, which is dedicated to the memory of those who gave their lives. It is my belief that Rotherham people who lived and died through the years of the Great War must not be forgotten.

This book is a small attempt to bring just a few of those personalities back to life. This book is dedicated to their memory, but most of all, this book is written:

TO COMMEMORATE THE MEN OF ROTHERHAM
WHO DURING THE GREAT WAR 1914 – 1918
GAVE THE MOST THAT LOVE CAN GIVE
LIFE ITSELF
FOR GOD, FOR KING, FOR COUNTRY
AND THE FREEDOM OF THE WORLD

Inscription on the Cenotaph in Clifton Park, Doncaster Road, Rotherham

CHAPTER 1

War clouds gather

In 1914 the people of Rotherham, like many other towns, were apprehensive of the war clouds that threatened its peace. Little could be gleaned from newspapers that war was fast approaching. May Day in Rotherham resulted in almost wintry weather, which had dampened some of the traditional celebrations. A correspondent to the *Rotherham Advertiser* of 2 May noted that, traditionally, the people of the town would 'walk into the fields and rejoice his spirit with the sweet savour of the flowers and the harmony of the birds'. Now there was so much industry in the town that instead 'men walk into mines, forges and workshops and see nothing of flowers and birds'.

Thankfully the weather improved by August, in time for the Bank Holiday. Up to that point trade in the town had improved so much that it was estimated that most people had sufficient money to enjoy the holiday festivities. The railway companies laid on plentiful excursions to local beauty spots, and it was anticipated that people who could afford it 'would leave the town in an exodus'. Others took their holidays in Clifton Park, Boston Park and the nearby ruins of Roche Abbey. Although few Rotherham people could be unaware that the political situation was deteriorating, the local papers claimed that 'little panic or alarm was visible on the faces of the town's population'. Nevertheless, after months of speculation, on 4 August 1914 it was finally announced that a state of war existed between Britain and Germany.

At the very first council meeting held after the announcement, the lord mayor, Alderman P. Bancroft Coward, told his colleagues:

Since the council met a month ago war clouds have gathered over Europe, and also unfortunately over the British Isles and today we find ourselves at war with Germany. It is a most serious and momentous time for the king and his ministers, and it is incumbent upon us that we should all be a united body. It is our duty to help the king and his ministers all we can by keeping cool and collected, but with brave and stout hearts, determined to undergo any deprivation which may be necessary; and to resist our enemies to the utmost of our might. We must have confidence in our God and trust that He will protect our king and country from our foes. God save the king.

What was unknown at the time was that in the ensuing conflict thousands of Rotherham men would die in what was to become known as the Great War. Indeed the war was only twenty-four hours old when news was heard about the very first victim. He was Ernest Jubb, who had lived with his parents at Clifton Grove, Rotherham. He was a sailor with HMS *Amphion*, when a mine hit the ship on 5 August 1914 at 6.30am, while most of the crew were still having breakfast. The captain ordered his men to abandon ship and the sailors in the water could only look on with horror as the ship, still under momentum, was struck by a second mine just a half-an-hour later. HMS *Amphion* took just fifteen minutes to sink after the second explosion, but thankfully many of the crew were rescued, although Ernest was not among them. His family, hearing the news of the sinking of the ship, immediately contacted the Admiralty, where his death was confirmed on the morning of Monday 10 August. It was reported the following week that the Jubb family, consisting of both his parents, two other sons and one daughter, had been inundated with sympathetic messages and letters of condolence from friends and family.

Meanwhile in Rotherham, despite this early tragedy, the enlistment process went into full swing. Posters were quickly erected throughout the town and the mayor, in his position of chief magistrate of the county borough, appealed to all eligible men to enlist. The posters requested that men:

... respond to the call of your king and country in this hour of national trial [...]The present fateful emergency is the greatest crisis your country has ever been faced with, and you are needed to play your part in maintaining the empire.

Other posters appeared, from the infamous poster showing Lord Kitchener himself stating 'Your Country Needs You' to the stirring 'Call to Arms'. These would have greatly excited the young men of the town, who were eager to enlist in a war that was only expected to last for six months. Many men living in the districts scattered all around the town were also desperate not to miss the opportunity of going abroad to fight, and motor buses were employed to drive them into Rotherham town centre. Local collieries and businesses encouraged workmen to enlist, assuring them that jobs would be kept open for them. Some employers gave bounties to men who went to join the colours.

Many who enlisted were placed into local battalions made up almost entirely of people from the same area or workplace, which became known as Pals Brigades. They enlisted in their thousands into the King's Own Yorkshire Light Infantry and the West Riding Infantry, but the battalion that recruited most Rotherham men was the York and Lancaster Regiment. The war diary of the regiment announced on the very day that war had been declared that:

an order to mobilise had been received and 896 notices to join were sent out from the headquarters in Rotherham.

Recruitment offices were also opened but within days St George's Hall on College Street was unable to cope with the demand and another office was quickly opened on Percy Street. As the officers struggled to deal with the queues of men, within days there were complaints about the slowness of the process. On 10 August the chief constable of Rotherham, Mr E. Weatherhogg, was requested to appoint a man to be stationed at the office on Percy Street from 10am to 1pm and 2pm to 5pm every day. His orders were 'to maintain order and to assist generally' in dealing with all the people waiting to enlist. In order to accommodate the large numbers of men on 6 August, the war diary stated that 'the men went into billets at the St Ann's and Doncaster Road Schools'.

Percy Street as it is today

On 10 August, just six days after war had been declared, the war diary notes that the York and Lancaster battalion based at Rotherham already had a total of twenty-eight officers and 876 other ranks. Most battalions were at that time based with cavalry units and, therefore, horses were also donated or requisitioned from local people. The diary also notes that forty-seven horses were with the newly enlisted troops, as the battalion moved to Doncaster for training. Sadly many of these horses would die before they ever reached France, being shoved together into cattle trucks totally unsuitable for the cargo they would be carrying.

At Doncaster, the Rotherham men who had enlisted with the York and Lancaster Regiment, found tents and bivouacs set up for them on the racecourse. These camps prepared the soldiers for war, with basic training in marching to improve the men's physical fitness, and familiarising the men in the use of field artillery. The war diary records that in order to complete their training, on 4 September the men were marched to Sandbeck Park, a distance of 12 miles. Meanwhile, rapid enlistment continued in Rotherham, and over the next few days the battalion at Doncaster was swollen by the addition of ninety more other ranks and six more horses. The following month another 175 recruits joined the regiment at Sandbeck Park for training. By November, a novel recruitment scheme was noted in Rotherham, at the Empire and Hippodrome theatres. Before each performance recruitment sergeants climbed onto the stage and, to packed audiences, would give a rousing five-minute speech encouraging men to enlist.

Sadly it was not long before news came to Rotherham about soldiers of the town being reported as killed, wounded or missing. On Wednesday 2 December 1914, Mrs Arnell of Wortley Road, Thorpe Hesley, was informed that her youngest son, Clement Arnell, aged 31, had been killed in action. He had lived at home with his widowed mother after serving for five years with the police force in Bishop Auckland. On returning to Rotherham, Private Arnell had been a reservist with the Coldstream Guards and rejoined his regiment on the outbreak of the war. The local newspaper reported that he was the first soldier from Thorpe Hesley to have been killed.

Empire Theatre as it is today

A typical funeral in a German prison-of-war camp during the Great War

The newspaper also requested information on Private Enoch Brooke who was reported as missing. He had been serving since August with his battalion the 2nd Duke of Wellingtons, West Riding Regiment. Private Brooke was the adopted son of Mrs Brooke of Atlas Street, Canklow, and she had just been informed that he had been wounded 'at a place unknown', but nothing else was known about him. Months later she learned that Private Brooke had been captured during the Battle of Mons and was taken to Wittenburg camp on the Elbe. Only after the war, when thankfully he returned to Rotherham, did Mrs Brooke find out that the same month she received the news he was a prisoner, an epidemic of typhus had hit the camp, which decimated the prisoners already weak through lack of diet and overcrowding. It seems that the prisoners were forced to take care of each other as the German doctors left and before British doctors from other camps were gradually drafted in. Food was unobtainable and the prisoners died like flies with the other prisoners holding funerals for their former comrades. Private Brooke told his mother that the men had only been saved by receiving the Red Cross parcels.

Some good news was received by Mrs May in February 1915, from her husband Private W. May of Charles Street, Thornhill, Rotherham. He had been called up as a reservist in August 1914 with his regiment the King's Own Yorkshire Light Infantry. Private May had also been involved in the retreat from Mons and the battles at Aisne and Belgium. In a letter to his wife, dated 12 February 1915, he told her not to worry as he was taking care of himself as much as he could. He revealed his wish to get back to Rotherham as he wrote:

I think I am as a good as any German when I have my rifle in my hand. At any rate, I have proved it so up to now. War is war and you never know your luck. What we want now is some warm weather, because it is so cold in the trenches. It will be much better when we get some warm weather here, and then I think it [the war] will not last very long. Let us hope that it will not, so that we can all come home again to our wives and kiddies. I am sure we all want to get home. We have had plenty of bad weather these last three months.

Stories circulated in the town and there was much curiosity about the instruments of war. On 8 July 1915, people were excited to hear that two German Howitzers, abandoned by the enemy due to the mud, were to be brought to Rotherham and placed on display. The war diary reports that Captain Colver ordered that one of these captured guns was to be transported to Rotherham to be placed in the drill hall there. In October 1915, several other interesting war curios that had been sent direct from the trenches were displayed in the windows of Mr A. S. Brittain of Henry Street. These gruesome relics included German, French and British service bayonets, hand grenades, German cartridges, etc, as well as a German helmet, a Pickelhaube and field glasses.

As more soldiers in khaki were seen around the town, the morals of women and young girls were quickly brought into question. Reports appeared in the local press about giddy girls becoming infatuated with the men in uniform. The billeting, training and drilling of soldiers, of necessity, had to be carried out in large halls and, very quickly the two larger buildings of the town, the drill hall and St George's Hall were adapted for use. Being practically in the centre of town it is not surprising that 'a lot of interest was being paid to the men during their parades and training'. As early as 4 December 1914, the Rotherham chief constable, Mr Weatherhogg, informed his men that:

> ... special attention be paid to the young women and girls found in the neighbourhood where the soldiers are being billeted [...]. Girls' names, ages and addresses should be made and the matter reported to me.

He requested that particular attention be paid to 'women of known immoral character', who had also been seen in the area. Despite the vigilance of the police constables, the matter simply intensified. On 1 July 1915, Major Rhodes, who trained the men at the drill hall, complained once again about 'the special attention that was paid to the soldiers from the women of the town'. He said that women and girls were gathering at 9.30am and 2.30pm specifically to watch the men parading and also at 1pm and 5pm

A replica of a World War I German helmet

World War One binoculars

when the men took their meals. On 29 July 1915, the claim was made again that not only were women of doubtful character frequenting the area around the drill hall, but they were also congregating in nearby Clifton Park. Once again the chief constable told his men that they must keep a strict watch for these women, and particularly when they were accompanied by soldiers.

The gates of Clifton Park, Rotherham, as they look today

More complaints followed that these same women were hanging around the YMCA tent that had been erected in Clifton Park in June 1915. This was a large tent provided by the British Women's Temperance Association and was opened by the mayor on 11 June. In his opening speech the mayor stated:

> it was now recognised that the more sober and purer life that men in the army led, the more efficient an instrument he would be for the welfare of the nation. It was with these aims that the tent had been supplied.

Non-alcoholic refreshments were also provided in the tent and this was where men could write letters homes on free paper and envelopes. Police constables were asked to visit the tent late at night and early in the mornings, and they were instructed that any women found in the tent had to be brought straight to the police station. Mr Weatherhogg must have felt he was losing the battle when the following month he learned that matters had not improved. Resignedly he ordered that if women were found to be regularly associating with soldiers, they were to be told in no uncertain terms to clear off. The chief constable also warned that any young girls under the age of 16 found with soldiers must be reported immediately to himself.

Complaints continued to be made to the police and the military authorities, and such a scandal was developing that the *Advertiser* took up the campaign and complained in June 1915 that:

> ... these girls are more to blame than the soldiers on who they literally throw themselves. If they cannot save themselves, and their parents can't save them, then the civil and military authorities should take action and punish them.

Incredibly the authorities became so alarmed at the situation that a committee was formed in the early months of 1915 to look into 'the morals of the young people of Rotherham'. They presented their findings in April and stated that although the morals of the town were no worse than other towns in the district, their enquiries had thrown up several serious concerns. They had found that since the war began there had been a reduction in the moral behaviour of young people of the town exacerbated by:

- The prevalence of the practice of young people promenading the streets of the town without definite purpose
- The frequency of hasty marriages, for which one reason only can be informed

The committee were unanimous that the co-operation of the parents, or those who 'have influence over such young people', should have the matter brought to their attention. Gravely warning that the best 'bulwark against the danger of immorality is undoubtedly the influence of a good home and the will and firm control of parents', the committee pointed out:

> It is a grave responsibility to bring children into a world full of temptations, but it is a great joy to see them growing stronger by reason of temptation resisted. It is wrong, however, to let them run into temptation, especially at an age when they do not fully realise the consequences that ensue. We appeal therefore to all parents to earnestly shoulder their responsibilities, to protect their children from running into danger, and to build up around them a bright and happy home life.

As the war went on, however, some women found that there were not enough men in khaki. Female vigilantes had been known to hand out white feathers as a sign of cowardice to able bodied young men not seen in uniform on the streets of Rotherham. One man who received such a white feather was Lance Corporal Sydney James, who had up to the outbreak of war led a charmed life as a professional footballer. He lived at Wharf Road, Tinsley, which at that time came within the boundary of Rotherham with his widowed mother Sarah. The 1911 census shows that at that time his mother was 57 and they shared the

Sarah James	Head		57	Widow
Tom James	Son	29		Single
Sydney James	Son	20		Single
Frank James	Son	17		Single
Martha James	Daughter		13	

The 1911 Census showing the family of Lance Corporal Sydney James

An Agreement made the _25th_ day of _November_ 1913 between ARTHUR FAIRCLOUGH, of 6, Doncaster Road, Barnsley, in the County of Yorkshire, the Secretary of and acting pursuant to Resolution and Authority for and on behalf of the HUDDERSFIELD TOWN ASSOCIATION FOOTBALL CLUB, LTD., of Leeds Road, Huddersfield, in the County of Yorkshire, (hereinafter referred to as the Club) of the one part and _Sidney James_ of _11 Wharf Road, Tinsley, Sheffield_ in the County of _Yorks_ Professional Football Player (hereinafter referred to as the Player) of the other part **Whereby** it is agreed as follows:

1. The Player hereby agrees to play in an efficient manner and to the best of his ability for the Club during the season 191_3_-191_4_

2. The Player shall attend the Club's ground or other place decided upon by the Club for the purposes of or connection with his training as a Player pursuant to the instructions of the Secretary, Team Manager, or Trainer, of the Club or of such other person or persons as the Club may appoint.

3. The Player shall do everything necessary to get and keep himself in the best possible condition prior to and during the season aforesaid so as to render the best possible service to the Club and shall carry out all the training and other instructions of the Club through its representative officials.

4. The Player shall observe and be subject to all the Rules Regulations and Bye-laws of the Football Association, the Football League, the Southern League and any other Association League or Combination of which the Club shall be a member.

The Football Agreement between Sydney James and Huddersfield Town Association Football Club

house with his two brothers, Tom aged 29 and Frank aged 17, and a sister, Martha, aged 13. Sydney had played as an amateur footballer for the Tinsley Church football team, as well as his local pub the Bird in Hand. On 28 November 1913 he was signed up by Huddersfield Town Association Football Club as a professional football player on wages of £2.10s a week. In order to keep him in the team when hostilities broke out, the club found him a job at a local steelmaking manufacturers called Hatfield's, which at that time was a reserved occupation. However, when Sydney received a white feather in 1916, he decided to enlist in the 9th Battalion of the King's Own Yorkshire Light Infantry. Sadly, Lance Corporal Sydney James was killed on Easter Monday 9 April 1917 on the opening day of what was to be known as the Battle of Arras. Seventy-two other soldiers also died in that battle, which was said to be one of the bloodiest battles of the war. Sydney and the other men of his regiment were buried in the Cojeul

Sydney James' grave in the Cojeul British cemetery

British cemetery and his name is also on the war memorial at Tinsley. His widowed mother never forgot his death and she kept the identity bracelet as a reminder of her footballer son to the day she died.

As more news came into Rotherham, it didn't take long before young men realised that warfare was not the glorified battle portrayed in stories of heroes. Modern warfare was brutal and conditions were dire, and few people in the town would predict that the war would last nearly five years.

Sydney James' identity bracelet, kept by his mother

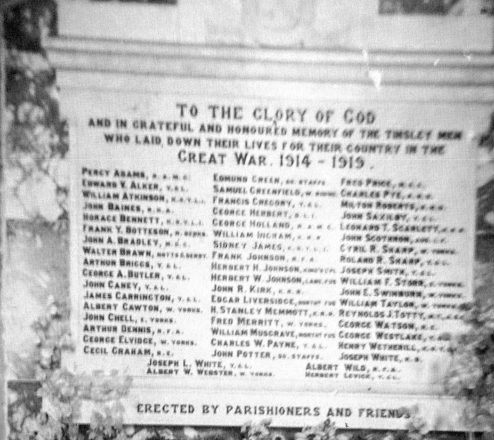

TO THE GLORY OF GOD
AND IN GRATEFUL AND HONOURED MEMORY OF THE TINSLEY MEN
WHO LAID DOWN THEIR LIVES FOR THEIR COUNTRY IN THE
GREAT WAR. 1914 - 1919.

PERCY ADAMS, R.A.M.C.   EDMUND GREEN, SO. STAFFS.   FRED PRICE, M.C.C.
EDWARD V. ALKER, Y.&L.   SAMUEL GREENFIELD, W. RIDING   CHARLES PYE, A.B.C.
WILLIAM ATKINSON, R.A.V.L.I. FRANCIS GREGORY, Y.&L.   MILTON ROBERTS, R.A.C.
JOHN BAINES, R.A.A.   GEORGE HERBERT, D.L.I.   JOHN SAXELBY, Y.&L.
HORACE BENNETT, R.A.V.L.I.   GEORGE HOLLAND, R.A.M.C.   LEONARD T. SCARLETT, R.A.A.
FRANK Y. BOTTERON, W. BERKS. WILLIAM INGRAM, K.R.R.   JOHN SCOTKBON, ARM. C.F.
JOHN A. BRADLEY, M.&C.   SIDNEY JAMES, K.O.Y.L.I.   CYRIL R. SHARP, W. YORKS.
WALTER BRAWN, NOTTS & DERBY. FRANK JOHNSON, R.F.A.   ROLAND R. SHARP, Y.&L.
ARTHUR BRIGGS, Y.&L.   HERBERT H. JOHNSON, KING'S CO. JOSEPH SMITH, Y.&L.
GEORGE A. BUTLER, Y.&L.   HERBERT W. JOHNSON, LANC. FUS WILLIAM F. STORR, C. YORKS.
JOHN CANEY, Y.&L.   JOHN R. KIRK, K.R.R.   JOHN E. SWINBURN, W. YORKS.
JAMES CARRINGTON, Y.&L.   EDGAR LIVERSIDGE, NORTH'D FUS WILLIAM TAYLOR, W. YORKS.
ALBERT CAWTON, W. YORKS.   H. STANLEY MEMMOTT, K.R.R.   REYNOLDS J. TOTTY, R.F.A.C.
JOHN CHELL, E. YORKS.   FRED MERRITT, W. YORKS.   GEORGE WATSON, R.E.
ARTHUR DENNIS, R.F.A.   WILLIAM MUSGRAVE, NORTH'D FUS GEORGE WESTLAKE, Y.&L.
GEORGE ELVIDGE, W. YORKS.   CHARLES W. PAYNE, Y.&L.   HENRY WETHERILL, K.R.V.&L.
CECIL GRAHAM, R.E.   JOHN POTTER, SO. STAFFS.   JOSEPH WHITE, R.E.

JOSEPH L. WHITE, Y.&L.   ALBERT WILD, R.F.A.
ALBERT W. WEBSTER, W. YORKS.   HERBERT LEVICK, Y.&L.

ERECTED BY PARISHIONERS AND FRIENDS.

Tinsley War Memorial, where Sydney James' name is engraved

CHAPTER 2

The realities of warfare

Modern historians are aware that behind the propaganda and jingoism of the Great War the realities of warfare were a shock to most soldiers who enlisted. In Rotherham some early reports of the war described vividly some of the horrors that awaited them. One letter illustrated how the condition of the trenches and the constant explosion from the shells resulted in a decision that any regiment would only spend a few days fighting on the front line before being relieved. Corporal J. A. Ward wrote to the editor of the *Advertiser* describing how on 24 November 1914 his battalion, the 2nd Lifeguards, were relieving the 3rd Dragoon Guards in the trenches. One of the men he had been relieving told Corporal Ward that on 21 November they had been shelled almost continually. When the shells finally stopped and in the quiet that followed, the Germans, thinking they had wiped everybody out in the French and British trenches, advanced over No-Man's-Land. As they approached the wire, the 3rd Dragoons opened fire and the unnamed soldier described to Corporal Ward how his regiment shot the enemy down. He told him:

The German wounded was all around us and it was horrible. The French, who were on our right, got out of the trenches in the middle of the night to look what unit they belonged to, and found they were the Prussian Guard. About nine o clock on the 22nd they let us have it again [...]It was awful, the trenches kept falling in and partially burying the wounded. We could not move them until it got dark, and when we got them to our communication trench the Germans kept shelling us while we were dressing their wounds.

Corporal Ward described how, when his regiment were finally relieved, the men had to march 4 miles away from the Front to get to their billet. He told the editor the men were so tired they kept falling into shell holes and they passed dead bodies lying in the road. Describing the gruesome relics, Corporal Ward said that some remains consisted of just random arms and legs, whilst other bodies were whole and some completely headless. Finally, when they reached the safety of a nearby town, the men were able to relax from the noise of the shelling. There Corporal Ward stated that they were supplied with fresh underclothing and able to have a shave, and soon they felt like new men. Concluding his letter, he said that for a few days his battalion had a lovely big hall to sleep in and stables for the horses, and it seemed so nice after being in the trenches day after day. The *Rotherham Advertiser* continued throughout the remainder of the war to realistically report the conditions on the battlefields. Yet this did not deter the still patriotic Rotherham people who continued to flock to recruitment offices to enlist.

By May 1915, two more Rotherham men confirmed the terrible conditions at the Front. Private William Henry Connelly of Mexborough had joined the York and Lancaster regiment and had been wounded near Ypres on Saturday 8 May 1915. He wrote a letter to his father stating that he had been brought back to a VAD hospital in West Malling, Kent, to recover from his wounds. Whilst there he dismissed those who predicted the war would be over soon, as he told his father:

I can tell you I am not sorry to get away from that country, as it is not warfare, but pure murder. I can tell you it won't be over for twelve months yet.

Another soldier named Private Isaac Greenwood also described conditions in France, stating 'this is not what is called war, it is pure slaughter' in a letter that he wrote to his mother, who lived in School Street, Eastwood View, Rotherham. Private Greenwood told her that in places there was only 10 to 15 yards of No-Man's-Land between his battalion and the enemy. When it was very quiet they could hear the Germans talking in their trenches. He ended his letter by echoing the thoughts of thousands of fighting men when he stated 'I wish it was all over'. Unfortunately, Private Greenwood, who was an eldest son, was one of the many who died. His mother was informed two years later on 23 April 1917 that he had been killed in action. Another letter written in May 1915 from Private J. Molineaux of the 1st battalion York and Lancaster Regiment was sent to the *Advertiser*. He was recovering from wounds in the Scottish General Hospital when he stated that he had witnessed the death of Private G. Campsall in the trenches, a few miles from Ypres. Whilst not going into detail about his death he added: 'suffice it to say that he was a Rotherham lad who died like a true British soldier.' Private Molineaux asked for more men from the town to enlist and:

> *Let them picture Rotherham as I have seen streets in Belgium, mown dead woman and children lying dead in the streets, some buried in the houses in which they lived. This is no fairy tale; this is what I actually saw at Ypres.*

In the years of the Great War there was little understanding of what effects the terrible conditions would have on ordinary men from places

German soldiers in the trenches whose voices could be heard across No-Man's-Land

like Rotherham. Formerly peaceful men, who prior to the war had been working on farms and in factories and mines, were now expected to actively shoot at other men. Some soldiers recognised the thrill of battle whilst at the same time acknowledging the losses. When Sergeant W. Finnie of the 1st Cameron Highlanders was wounded and in the 4th Scottish General Hospital in Glasgow, he wrote to his sister who lived in Rotherham. He told her of his very exciting escape from the battle at Aisne the previous month where he says:

> *There were thousands of Germans, and to make it worse, they had*

their artillery guns trained on us and they just mowed our poor fellows down. This went on for a little while and we were in a complete trap, and I am very sorry to say that very few of us got out of it. To tell you the truth I had given up all hope of coming home again.

He told her that out of his section of twenty men there were only three left alive and all of those had been wounded. These letters from the front line describing atrocities the soldiers were forced to witness was backed up by accounts in the York and Lancaster war diary. Colonel Wyllie reports that on the night of 12 June 1917:

The 5th King's Own Yorkshire Light Infantry carried out a raid on the enemies trenches opposite Neuve Chapelle where three companies took part. They succeeded in entering the enemies front and support lines and obtaining identification and killing large numbers of enemy. No prisoners were taken. [5]

The enemy were swift to retaliate. At 2.48am at a part of the front line where the 'trench line was not accurately known', the Germans reached a trench occupied mainly by the same battalion and in turn left twenty British soldiers dead. Sergeant Frank Carpenter also wrote a letter to the editor of the *Advertiser* echoing the feelings of many men:

This war is a terrible thing and I know there is not a man who will not be glad when it is over, although he is fighting keen enough. I know I shall be jolly glad when it stops, if God spares me to the end. He has spared me so far, and I pray He will do so until it is all finished. I should not weep if it was to end this minute, although I am glad I came.

There is a clear impression that he speaks for a generation, who even though they went to war and put up with the awful conditions, that would not have missed it for the world.

But perhaps the biggest effect that the war had on Rotherham was in the Battle of the Somme, which became known as the big push and which started on 1 July 1916. It was thought by the military authorities that bombarding the Germans for several days and nights would weaken their defences, leaving it clear for a British victory and thereby end the war. But the manoeuvre failed and it is a matter of record that

A shell hole dating from the Great War in Ypres today

thousands of Rotherham men were killed on that day. All that was left of these heavy bombardments are the large shell holes that still exist today.

The lead-up to the battle is recorded in the York and Lancaster war diary. The entry for 26 June, states that the military authorities had ordered there was to be the utmost secrecy regarding the date that the battle would commence. Consequently the first battle of the Somme would be referred to as Z day.

On what was then renamed Y day, 27 June, the men were visited by Commander General Percival, who presented medals and spoke encouragingly to the whole battalion. 'All the preparations have been completed, except that a few steel helmets were short.' Unfortunately by 4.30pm the order was cancelled due to the heavy rain and it was renamed 'Y day-2'. According to the diary, the next day, Y/1, the preparations continued as the battalion marched to the assembly trenches at Aveluy Wood. Finally on Z day the bombardment of shells commenced at 9.45am near Thiepval Wood, and was so terrible, that for three days the area resulted in 'bodies, kit and equipment strewn all over the tracks and trenches'.

When news reached Rotherham of the large numbers of local soldiers killed, the newspapers were filled with reported deaths. One of the first was that of Private Bert Greenwood of Holmes Lane, Rotherham, who died of wounds received on 1 July 1916. He was the second son of Mr and Mrs Walter Greenwood and before he enlisted had worked in the grocery section of the Masbrough Co-op Society. Private Greenwood was also a well-known member of the Rotherham Thursday Football Club, where he was described as:

> [...] being a clever player in the position of centre forward, who had scored many goals. He had broken his leg twice whilst playing football and had won a medal as part of Ferham Council School Football Team.

When war broke out, Private Greenwood joined the York and Lancaster Regiment in the early days. Sadly, when he was killed in action he was

The Masbrough Co-operative Society building on left of the picture, now a nightclub

only 22 years of age and left a young widow. What might be the worst result of the big push, however, was the large number of local men reported missing and never found. One was Private Frank B. Oldham, a machine-gunner of the York and Lancaster regiment. He had lived at Kenneth Street, Rotherham, where it was reported that his wife and six children were anxiously still waiting for news at the end of September of that same year. Despite the fact that his body was never found, his name is inscribed on the war memorial in Clifton Park.

Thankfully some soldiers who had been reported as missing did eventually turn up. Rifleman Robert Preston of the King's Royal Rifles was not only reported as missing, following the 1 July battle, but had also been officially reported as killed. Thankfully, on 9 September 1916, a letter was received by his family to say he had been in a German hospital in France. He wrote: 'I am now in a convalescent hut in some prison camp in south Germany, and whilst here I have had some decent soups, so at present I am not doing so badly.' Describing his capture he stated that:

The enemy blew a mine and as I am a bomber, I threw three bombs and then received thirty wounds in my left side from some of their grenades. Needless to say I was helpless, and then three men surrounded me. It was an easy matter for them to drag me 50 yards to their trench. I was taken to a dug out 30 feet underground, and my wounds were immediately dressed and I was put to bed. They gave me cognac and plenty of coffee.

As the sad news was discussed in the town a reporter stated that 'during the past few weeks, the graves of many of the soldiers have been found, and the worst fears of their families have been realised'. The *Advertiser* stated that 'July 1st 1916 will be long remembered as a blood-red letter-day for the Rotherham district, as well as a day of glorious deeds'.

Writing to a close relative of a man killed in battle was never an easy task for a battalion commander or a comrade, but it was hoped that a personal observation and re-assurance that the soldier had died quickly and without pain was helpful to parents. In September 1916, news was heard of the death of another soldier missing since 1 July. The body of Signaller Horace Keyworth of Kimberworth Road, Rotherham, was found by members of his battalion of the York and Lancaster regiment.

One of his comrades, Private H. A Winders, wrote a letter to his parents, dated 22 September:

> *I am writing to tell you how extremely sorry all your dear son's comrades were, to hear the sad news which was brought to us today. His body was found and buried by a chaplain of HM Forces in the field a few days ago, so you will see he had a Christian burial. He was well-known and well-loved by every man in the battalion. The corporal and all the signallers of the section to which Horace was attached, speak of their great regrets. Horace was one of the most cheerful and kind in the regiment. He did not seem to know what fear was, and his death is a great loss to us. I sincerely hope that you will look to God above to give you strength to bear this terrible news.*

One of the main realities of warfare, however, was largely ignored and usually only revealed in letters home to loved ones, was simply the fact that men at the front line didn't want to be there. In true patriotic fashion they had gone to war to serve king and country, but when they got to France and other battlefields all they wanted was to be at home with their families. One such Rotherham soldier was Samuel Maiden, who wrote heartfelt letters to his wife, Rose Elizabeth, who he called Lizzie, at their house on Clay Pit Lane, Sandhill, Rawmarsh. Samuel had been in the army prior to the outbreak of war under his own name, when his beloved daughter Rosie was born in 1912. Little is known about his army service up to this point, but it was known in the family that he went AWOL in order to see his newly born daughter. Luckily he managed to evade the military authorities, who were no doubt looking for him. Nevertheless, when war broke out, Samuel was intent on doing his duty and, risking the chance of being court-marshalled, he enlisted under the name of Private F. G. Ernscliffe. He joined the 2nd Life Guard battalion of the 13th Hussars. The letters he sent home are almost a century old. Nevertheless, they clearly reveal the feelings of a man who, although he was doing his duty, just wanted to be at home with his wife and child.

Although many of the letters are not dated, in what appears to be the first letter, he writes to Lizzie to let her know that he had 'arrived here alright, but I shall not settle till I get back to you'. His agony comes out in his words as he describes his depression:

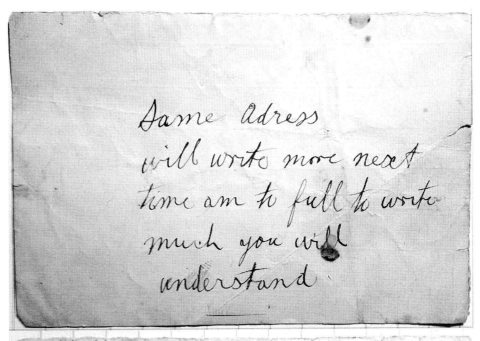

Same Adress
will write more next
time am to full to write
much you will
understand

all I can say I feel as
though I dont want to
do anything sit and
think of you all day long
I am on guard to night
well I will close now

Samuel Maiden's letter home to his wife Lizzie saying that he just wants to 'sit and think of you all day long'.

Same address will write more next time [I] am too full to write much, you will understand [...] all I can say I feel as though I don't want to do anything [but] sit and think of you all day long.

The letters also give an indication of long hours of boredom, which the men of his unit filled by singing. The 2nd Life Guard Battalion was a cavalry unit and Samuel wrote that the men would sing *Hold Your Hand Out, You Naughty Boy* whilst they groomed the horses in the cavalry depot of the Richmond Barracks in Dublin. In a later letter he tells Lizzie that he wished he had a photograph of 'you and our Rosie, I could keep having a look at it'. Samuel also complains of the boredom of waiting for orders to come:

I expect they will come some of these days and we shall be packed off straight away. I should just like to see you once more before I go out. I expect we shall in the end, and I shall be pleased when this is over'.

Meanwhile, Samuel complains about the military authorities, as he tells his wife: 'They are all running in the same old groove, nothing doing. Sometimes getting ready to move and the next minute the orders are cancelled.' He enviously tells her that 'two regiments left Dublin yesterday, the West Kents and the Scottish Borders, but where they went nobody knows'. In a later letter he asks whether she has received her separation allowance from the paymaster at York yet. Samuel tells her that some of the soldiers' wives in his unit had received theirs, whereas others hadn't. Once again he complains about his surroundings:

I am still at the same old dirty Dublin, I shall be glad when I am with you again in Rotherham. I should have liked you to have been here the other day. There are about 300 Reserves of all Hussars Regiments here, and they were all sat outside the canteen drinking and everyone had to sing. There were some fine singers among them. We had a grand do I can tell you.

Despite the fact that Samuel had enlisted under an assumed name, it seems that the military authorities were complicit in the deception in order for his separation money to be paid to his wife. One letter, simply dated 'Dublin 15th', which might possibly be 15 August, tells her he had received his birth certificate all right. He writes:

> *I don't see any reason why you should not put your name down. I expect you will hear from York. Anyway, they will send you our marriage lines back. Of course, I might have to remain in this name, and they might put you down as Mrs Ernscliffe on the army books.*

In one of the few letters dated 17 August 1914, Samuel admitted that he had suffered from a bad back but that the stiffness had now gone, through lying on the floor. He sadly regrets missing the early years of his daughter's life as he complains 'the way the war is going on, Rosie will be a big girl by the time I return'. Hopefully he tells Lizzie that he expects that the war will not last another six months.

Tragically in what must be the last letter that Samuel Maiden wrote, which was again undated but this time headed 'Aldershot', he enquires again whether she has received her separation allowance. He gently chides her for not writing and tells her:

> *I have not heard from you for over a week. I shall stop writing myself. It's bad enough me being away from you, but not getting a letter to let me know how you are getting on, makes things worse'.*

The chiding must have had the desired effect as the next letter is the only one from Lizzie to Samuel. She dated it 28 October 1914 and mentions a postcard she received the previous night. Lizzie tells him that she is longing for a letter because 'you can't put much on a postcard', and 'hopes that he has got some of her own letters by now'. She adds that she was 'going to send the postcard to your mother, to tell her I have heard from you as they are all longing to hear how you are, and I am pleased to think you are alright'. Lizzie goes on to describe a recent birthday party for Rosie, and all the presents that their child received, adding 'we only wanted you as well to finish it off, but I hope you will be here for the next'. Ending the letter 'from your loving wife' she adds eight kisses to the bottom. You can sense from the letter that she tries to cheer Samuel up, by adding 'don't be downhearted, think about coming back again'. Sadly there are no more letters. Samuel Maiden died of wounds on 16 November 1914 aged 33. That the military authorities were aware of the deception of his name is confirmed as the announcement of his death stated 'Samuel Maiden (served as Ernscliffe)'. His body was buried at Gent City Cemetery in Belgium where he was 'Remembered with Honour'. Lizzie thankfully went on to marry twice more and had four more children, but the fragile condition of the letters suggests that she never forgot her first husband and read them many times over the years until they almost dropped to bits in the process.

More than anything those few precious letters give a real insight to realities of war and the boredom of waiting to be sent to the Front. No doubt echoing the thoughts of many men who went away to fight, their thoughts were constantly with their loved ones at home.

The fragile condition of Samuel Maiden's letters

CHAPTER 3

Life in the trenches

It is a well-known fact that the early years of the Great War saw a stalemate in the trenches, which took the military authorities by surprise. It had been expected that great advances would be quickly made by British and allied troops, bringing the war swiftly to an end. In fact, little ground was taken and instead of being a temporary refuge,

The layout of the Great War trenches in Ypres today

trenches were where battalions spent the majority of their time. Some of these trenches changed hands many times and for a battalion to hold onto a trench was quite an achievement. One Rotherham soldier, Lance Corporal Rylett of the Duke of Cornwall's Light Infantry, wrote proudly to the editor of the *Advertiser* on 1 August 1915. He told him

Even today the Great War trenches need constant maintenance

that his regiment held the record for the length of time they managed to hold onto a trench. He and his comrades entered the trench on the night of 26 April 1915 and held it until 25 July, when his men were relieved by the Gordon Highlanders". These trenches needed constant repair and the war diary reports by May 1915 that night working parties of from between 100 – 250 men were repairing trenches under cover of darkness. This was very dangerous work as they often worked just 100 yards from the enemy and their ever more accurate snipers. As the war progressed, these trenches needed constant maintenance.

One of the main industries around Rotherham was coal mining and the military authorities quickly realised that experienced colliers would be essential to dig and maintain the trenches. In total around 217,000 men that enlisted to fight nationally were miners, and almost three quarters of those were from Yorkshire. Constant repair was needed as shelling blew each trench apart. German trenches were slightly more scientific in construction with the use of concrete, but they too had to mend and repair their trenches in any let-up of the shelling. By October 1915 the matter had not improved and the war diary records:

In front line trenches the weather was very bad, in consequences of which the trenches fell in in a large number of places, and also the communication trenches became flooded and almost impassable. The conditions regarding living were extremely bad

German soldiers constantly mending trenches in the Great War during a ceasefire

The waterlogged conditions in France in the Great War – note the carts abandoned due to the mud

> *and all ranks suffered very much from wet state of the trenches, and owing to the continuous rain very little work except clearing away falls of earth could be carried out'.*

Trenches were unhygienic places to live with hundreds of men living closely together in squalour. It was of necessity that latrines were within a very short distance of the trenches and on hot days the stench was unbearable. Despite heavy rainfall, the lack of clean water meant that men were unable to shave, keep themselves clean or even change their clothes. Vermin, including rats and mice, were prevalent, as well as decomposing bodies. The men in the trenches were also plagued with lice, which bred in the seams of their uniforms. Soldiers were forced to burn them out with matches, others would completely shave themselves to avoid infestation. They also had to deal with outbreaks

Great War trenches at Ypres today. Note the water still collecting in the bottom of the trench.

of influenza, scabies and other trench diseases. The war diary says that in January 1916, over fifty cases of scabies had been reported.[8] These were highly contagious outbreaks caused by tiny mites burrowing beneath the skin, and generally making life difficult.

An example of the many diseases soldiers could catch was taken from the service records of a stretcher-bearer named Private William Heywood. He was aged 29 years and 11 months when he enlisted with the York and Lancaster regiment on 5 September 1914. The casualty form on his record lists his illnesses while on active service, which are typical of the period. Private Heywood contracted influenza on 10 September 1915 and returned to his unit two days later. Only four days afterwards he contacted pyrexia and rejoined his unit on 20 September. The following year he reported sick with scabies in February before being sent to a hospital in Boulogne with an abscess in March. He was gassed in the early months of 1917 and only rejoined his unit in the spring of that year. Sadly Private Heywood was reported as missing in June 1917 and a letter was sent to his wife by one of the officers of his regiment. Lieutenant Vernon, wrote to his wife, in a rather brusque style:

> *I am sorry to tell you that your husband is missing. He went with me and the rest of the company on a raid on June 11th, where afterwards I found that some of the platoon was missing. One of them was your husband, so I am afraid that he is dead. We were unable to get all our dead, as we had the wounded to get in. One thing I am sure of was that he did his duty to the last. He was a great favourite of mine and I feel his loss very much.*

His effects were returned to his wife Marie on 22 May 1918 and to keep herself and four children she was awarded a pension of 28s 9d on 11 February 1918.

Another of the other terrible conditions the men in the trenches were subject to was frostbite. The military authorities had expected the war to be over by Christmas and therefore no protection had been given to soldiers enlisting in the first summer of the war. One Rotherham motor driver, Private E. Lawton, described the frosty conditions to his wife in a letter dated December 1914, where he used his own initiative in order to adapt to the conditions. He complained of cold in his hands and told her that he had found the perfect solution:

The weather is very cold here now, and a few days ago we had a heavy fall of snow followed by a keen frost. But the last day or two there has been a thaw and we have had some rain, so most of the snow has disappeared. We motor drivers find it very cold in our hands, as most of us came out without gloves in August. We never reckoned on a winter campaign and I myself wear a pair of socks which act very well

Some of the more serious cases of frostbite affected the feet as well as the hands and sometimes men had to be sent home to recuperate. One such soldier was Private P. Harpham, whose parents lived at Canklow Cottages. He was invalided home in April 1915 suffering from frostbitten feet, and he wrote a letter to his parents from a hospital at Sudbury in Suffolk. He was in a sombre mood as he told them that his condition was 'as well as could be expected' and that he was 'run down a little with the hardships we have gone through'. Urging his parents not to worry about him, Private Harpham told them 'I don't think it will be long before I am home again for a few days'. In a letter to his uncle he described how a shell had burst near him and the shrapnel had caught his feet and cut them before frostbite set in. He also told him that:

Three days ago I was in the trenches around Ypres, now I am in England so you see they are not long in getting you home when you are out of action.

One of the most acute conditions that affected the men in the trenches was caused by waterlogged conditions. When 'trench foot' was first noted by medical officers it was thought to be an illness brought on by poor morale. Only later was it established as a fungal condition caused by standing in trenches with feet immersed in water for hours on end. In order to combat the situation the men were issued with 'trench waders', which were rubber boots with high tops up to the waist, but these were quickly found to be useless. Instead of protecting men's feet they simply found themselves bogged down in the mud. One unnamed Greasbrough soldier writing to his mother in March 1917 stated that he had been wearing these boots, but before walking 200 yards:

They were half full of water and sludge, which will give you an idea of how deep the mud is out here [...] I had to get out of the trenches and go up on the top or I should have got stuck in the mud. One or two men were fast in the mud and their pals were trying to get them out. I set off again and all at once the enemy sent up a flare and down I went into a shell hole half full of water. Of course I wasn't alone, there was about four of us in all.

The waterlogged conditions at Ypres during the Great War in France

In order to combat the increasing prevalence of trench foot officers were ordered to regularly inspect the men's feet and soldiers were urged to keep their feet dry wherever possible. The less-serious cases could be treated while others became gangrenous and had to be amputated. Private Arnold Bray of Bear Tree Road, Parkgate, was one of these and he was moved from France to a hospital in Birmingham where he arrived for the operation on 23 December 1916. Private Bray was particularly unlucky as he had only been in France five weeks before he was diagnosed and sent back to England. By January 1917 it seems that the authorities were dealing better with the situation and that same month the York and Lancaster diary noted that 'cases of trench foot that month had been nil'. It was accounted for 'due to supplies of hot meals and drinks, and the removal of likely cases to the drying room at Bretancourt'.

But without doubt, the biggest killer that the men in the trenches had to contend with was the problems caused by gas attacks. From mid-1915, gas was frequently used by both sides. The early gas masks that were provided by the authorities were very primitive. The smell of the rubber caused soldiers to actually vomit inside the helmet, resulting in men flinging off their masks. Private J. Molineaux, who had been wounded, wrote a letter to the editor of the *Advertiser* in May 1915:

> *English soldiers are dying a most horrible death through the base use by the Huns of poisoned gases. I have seen men who have been gassed. I have seen them in torture and agony. What a relief it was to see them die, freed from the agony caused by these murderous Huns. My own wound which is a bullet through the face, although painful, is but a flea-bite compared to those suffering from gas.*

The war diary noted a particularly bad gas attack on the night of 19 December 1915, when a captain and two lieutenants were killed. In the same attack six other ranks were also killed and another eighty-seven were taken to the first aid post suffering from the effects of the gas. Many of the lucky ones that survived were taken to the rest camps to recuperate. But this caused depletion in the ranks and the war diary records a few days later that: 'The battalion feeling the effects of gas severely. Large majority suffering from bronchitis, caused by gas.'[10] When officers of the York and Lancaster regiment assessed the damage later, it was found that out of a total of 290 men over 100 were still very unwell. At first it was phosphorous gas that killed people, with symptoms similar to drowning on dry land. Later mustard gas was used to equally deadly effect.

The war diary records once again that on the night of 22 July 1917, a gas attack was noted, following the familiar smell of mustard and garlic. This gas was still new and the battalion had only just received a warning about it from the 5th Army that very morning. As a result, there was little understanding of its effects. After two full platoons had been evacuated as casualties, the officers noted that instead of dissolving, the gas continued to hang about in the trenches and the dugouts, making it extremely dangerous. As a result a total of 258 men suffered from the effects of just that one attack. The situation was so bad that a planned attack for the following night had to be cancelled, due to the condition of the troops. The diary recorded that even a month later, on 11 August, 144 men were still in hospital suffering from the effects received on the night of 22 July'.[11] One Rotherham soldier who died from the effect of that same gas attack was reported two months later on September 1917. Private Albert R. Berridge had been a reservist with the York and Lancaster Regiment and when war was declared, he was one of the first to be sent to France with the British Expeditionary Force. Private Berridge's bravery could not be questioned as he had been awarded the Royal Humane Society's certificate on 12 August 1912, when he rescued a boy from drowning

in the Greasbrough Dam. He was acting as a stretcher bearer and his relatives were informed of his death at Peasehill Street, Rawmarsh. Ultimately all the trenches were fitted with some kind of warning device, which could be sounded when gas was detected. The most common of these was an empty shell casing that could be banged loudly to announce the presence of gas. Nevertheless, despite attempts to counter the attacks, the primitive gas masks were so hot to wear and limited what could be seen, and many soldiers tore them off after only a few minutes and consequently died. Despite the fact that the use of poisonous gases was condemned in 1908, German troops were using them as early as October 1914.

Empty shell cases from World War one – which were later used to warn of gas attacks

The military authorities were beginning to recognise that life in the trenches for many was not only dangerous but also bad for morale. In order to combat the privations they ensured that the men would regularly be relieved. One Rotherham soldier, Private Tom Brailsford, formerly of Midland Road, Masbrough, was attached to the 2nd York and Lancaster regiment. He told his brother in February 1915 that men were now only serving 'four days in the trenches and four days in a rest camp'. The regimental diary record that a very different and longer 'rest camp' was tried in March 1916, when the battalion went to Candas in Northern France. As a complete breakaway from the trenches, the men were set to work on a damaged railway outside the town of Belle Eglise. For many months previously the men of the battalion had been subject to 'intense bombardment and shelling'. Parties of the men alternated with the work on the railway, whilst others underwent training, but all had access to baths, laundry and good food. The plan was a great success and it was reported on 31 March that the repairs on the line were almost finished and that:

German soldiers eating a meal during a lull in the shelling

Regular hours and full nights rest have worked wonders with the battalion. The slackness due to nearly a year of trench life is no longer apparent, and an entirely new stock of NCOs are beginning to find promise for the future.

However, such a break away from the fighting was very unusual, and all too soon the men returned back to the trenches.

Quite early in the war it was noted that the miners of Rotherham were not only crucial to digging the trenches but many of them were enlisted to specifically to dig tunnels under enemy lines. By February 1915, eight such companies of these tunnellers had been formed. These were highly skilled men, christened 'moles', who of necessity worked in absolute silence under enemy lines. Older men in their fifties with mining experience were quickly enlisted into these companies, where inevitably a heavy cloak of secrecy lay over their activities. The first mention of the tunnellers in the York and Lancaster diary was on 15 September 1916, when 'a composite company of 150 other ranks were delegated under B Company for the purpose of tunnelling under Thiepval'.

One Rotherham man who had trained as a mining engineer and was used as a 'mole' had served at the Treeton Colliery. He was Second Lieutenant Ronald Thomson, whose mother was a widow living at Melton House, Rotherham. He was 30 when he enlisted with the Royal Engineers, in the tunnelling section. He was described by some of his peers as being 'a popular and capable officer'. Naturally this was a very dangerous and difficult job, as the Germans were skilled at detecting tunnellers and blowing them up as they burrowed underground. So when Lieutenant Thomson was seriously wounded on 22 January 1917, his family were informed that he had received terrible injuries to his face, head and shoulders. Thankfully, word of his injuries reached his mother and brother at Rotherham in time for them to travel to the Lady Murray's Hospital at Le Treport France. Five days later he died from his wounds, but at least he had the comfort of having his mother and brother with him at the end.

The dangerous nature of tunnelling work and the need for secrecy meant that many former miners went unrecognised during the years of the Great War. Inevitably, however the dangers they faced on a daily basis could not be ignored. One of the first of the moles to be officially recognised for bravery was Corporal Enoch Dalton of Victoria Street, Maltby. He was also attached to the Royal Engineers and awarded a DCM in April 1915 for 'conspicuous gallantry and good work under very dangerous condition in changing and tamping mines within 5 feet of the enemy lines':

> *On April 1st 1915 at Cuinchy he crawled forward and surprised three Germans behind a sandbag barricade, and drawing them out. Thus enabled a charge to be laid and the gallery to be destroyed. On another night in June 21st 1915, in going down a mine and assisting in the rescue of four men under circumstances of great risk. On the morning of June 22nd the enemy exploded a mine which entombed nine men. Despite being affected by poisonous gas fumes, he went down the mine, time after time to rescue them'.*

The fascination with trench warfare started a trend that still continues

Great War shells still excavated at Ypres today

today. Many people go on regular tours to France to see the trenches where hundreds of men died. Long after the Great War finally ended the contents of the trenches and battlefields continue to interest military archaeologists today.

CHAPTER 4

Impact on family life

There is little doubt that the biggest impact the Great War had on the people of Rotherham was how it affected the lives of the families who were often ripped apart. Almost as soon as the war started news of deaths, relatives missing or wounded were heard on a daily basis. The fate of local men was often heard in the town before the official telegram from the war office confirmed the news. It is known from war diaries that roll calls were taken after battles, and as most of the battalions held a large contingency of soldiers from Rotherham, it is probable that news was passed on by comrades. For a relative the waiting must have seemed endless. There are some cases in Rotherham, however, when official notifications were delayed or not received by parents or widows.

In the case of Private Francis Percy Warren of Canklow, the confirmation was particularly important to his widow as the colliery where he previously worked had agreed to pay a sum of money when his death had been established. A letter was written on behalf of Mrs Warren from Mrs Ada Spicer reporting to the unknown recipient that the captain of Private Warren's unit had written to tell her of his death. In the letter, which was dated 9 July 1915, Mrs Spicer said that the colliery officials would not process the matter until official notice of his death had been received. A further letter was written, again on the behalf of Mrs Warren, from a man named Charles Longley, which was sent on 25 July 1915. Mr Longley stated that some of Private Warren's former comrades had also contacted her widow and confirmed her husband's death, although she still had no official notification. On 1 August yet another letter was sent requesting confirmation and also asking that 'for the sake of her husband' she would like his watch and other small items returned to her. The three letters underline not only the tragic loss that Mrs Warren had to deal with, and the anxious wait for the death to be confirmed, but also the financial problems she had to face. There is no resolution to the letters that were found in his service records, but the war diary records that Private Francis Warren was killed in the trenches on 18 June 1915 by a sniper.

Naturally the impact of the death of a beloved son was of enormous significance to grieving parents. Christopher Page sent details of his uncle, John William Page, who had been born in Wombwell, Barnsley, before moving with his parents Elizabeth and Francis to Whinney Hill, Rotherham. He was one of fifteen children and was born on

John William Page's Great War medal

2 February 1891. Private Page enlisted on 18 January 1915, aged 23, at Rotherham, where he was working as a collier. His father Francis was also serving in the labour battalion of the Royal Engineers. This was a specialised unit that built and maintained railways, engines and track vehicles in France, and his

family believe that he had enlisted at a later age due to some special skills that were needed for the war effort. Little research has been undertaken about the labour battalion of the Royal Engineers apart from the fact that there never seemed to be enough men recruited for this service.

After only ten weeks of training, on 31 May 1915, John William Page was drafted to the Dardanelles as part of the Plymouth battalion and he also served in Egypt for three months. Interestingly, his father Francis Page was discharged in March 1916 shortly after the Military Service Act was introduced. The authorities had decided that Conscientious Objectors were now to be used in the labour battalion. Francis Page returned to his home and his wife Elizabeth in

Francis Page in later years

BT 603538

CERTIFIED COPY   OF AN ENTRY
Pursuant to the Births and   Deaths Registration Act 1953

DEATH	Entry No. 26

| Registration district   Rotherham | Administrative area |
| Sub-district   Rotherham | Metropolitan District of Rotherham |

1. Date and place of death
   Twelfth April 1974
                 Thrybergh, Rotherham

| 2. Name and surname
Jack Hersin PAGE | 3. Sex   Male |
| | 4. Maiden surname
of woman who
has married |

5. Date and place of birth
   29th April 1918   Thrybergh, Yorks

6. Occupation and usual address
   Storekeeper (Oxygen Company)

7(a) Name and surname of Informant	(b) Qualification
	Present at the death
(c) Usual address.	

8. Cause of death
   I(a) Cardiac Infarction

   Certified by
   R E Price MB

| 9. I certify that the particulars given by me above are true to the best of my knowledge and belief | Signature
of informant |

| 10. Date of registration
            April 1974 | 11. Signature of registrar
     C H Tompkin Registrar |

Certified to be a true copy of an entry in a register in my custody.

Deborah Allex

*Superintendent Registrar
*Registrar

*Strike out whichever does not apply

Date 22nd April
        2005

CAUTION: THERE ARE OFFENCES RELATING TO FALSIFYING OR ALTERING A CERTIFICATE AND USING
OR POSSESSING A FALSE CERTIFICATE. °CROWN COPYRIGHT
WARNING: A CERTIFICATE IS NOT EVIDENCE OF IDENTITY.

The death certificate of Jack Hersin Page, who died at Rotherham in April 1974

Rotherham. Sadly Francis had only been home about three months when, on 22 June 1916, he was informed of the death of his son John William, who had received gunshot wounds in the left leg and also had a fractured left arm. Private John William Page died of his injuries the next day and was buried in a cemetery at Hersin, France. On 8 July the *South Yorkshire Times* gave tribute to him, remarking that since his enlistment, he had not had any home leave and never came back to Rotherham. Francis and Elizabeth never got over his death and when son Jack was born on 29 April 1918 they gave him the middle name of 'Hersin'.

Sadly there were many cases when the death of a soldier could not be confirmed as the body had not been found, and they were simply reported as missing. After thirty weeks the soldier was presumed to be killed in action. Another father, who all too well understood the situation, was Sapper William Henry Firth of Psalters Lane, Holmes. He had already served for a year with the Royal Engineers when he heard that his 20-year-old son, George Henry, had been officially reported as missing. When Sapper Firth requested information about his son's death a letter was received from the military authorities in October 1917 which stated:

> *It is with the utmost regret that I have to write and tell you that your son has been posted as missing and believed killed. From the information I have received I am sorry that I can give you very little hope of his being alive. His body has not yet been recovered [...] and the whole company, including the officers miss him very much, as he made many friends due to his unfailing cheerfulness under all conditions.*

Occasionally the military authorities got it wrong and the strange case of Private Richard Twigg was reported in November 1916. Private Twigg had been born at Masbrough, and ever since his parents had died, twelve years before war was declared, he lived with his brother and family at Wilfred Street, Westgate, Rotherham. Prior to joining the army he worked at Rotherham Main Colliery. Private Twigg was reported missing in the *Advertiser* on 4 November 1916. His family had received official notice of his death and they also received a card of sympathy from the king himself. However, thankfully he was very much alive and he wrote that he was 'at present still serving with his regiment at the Front'. He wrote to his relatives:

> *Dear brother, sisters and nephews and nieces*

Just a few lines hoping you are all well as it leaves me at present. I got the Advertiser the other week and I see they have got me down as killed! I have been to the Battalion Headquarters today and they say that I have got another man's number and the York and Lancaster's can't make it out. They have no Richard Twigg on their books. So it looks like me doing 26 months of service and no one knowing that I have enlisted!

Losing one son was bad enough, but the impact of losing two affected one family immensely. The service records that remain provide more information about the lives of soldiers and sailors in the Great War and they make fascinating reading. Thanks to information from relative Ann Mapplebeck, it was discovered that John Henry Beverley, a young man who was a bit of a rogue, which is borne out by his conduct sheets, lied about his age when he enlisted. This abuse of the enlistment system was uncovered quite early in the war where it was noted that some recruitment officers were not as scrupulous in checking the ages of recruits as they should be. Despite his perjury he was welcomed into the ranks of the 8th Battalion of the York and Lancaster Regiment on 31 August 1914, where he gave his age as 19 years and 10 months. Family research showed that in the 1911 census he was listed as only being 13 that year, which would mean that he was only 16 when he joined up. Nevertheless, the photograph we have of John illustrates his very young age. Gazing steadily at the camera we see a young man eager to 'do his bit' and probably, like many of that period, desperate to leave the town of his birth for the excitement of battle.

John's service records show that at the time he enlisted he still lived at home with his father George and his mother Adelaide Elizabeth Beverley at 66 Park Street, Rose Hill, Rawmarsh. Also sharing his parent's house were his two sisters, Mary Elizabeth aged 13 and Adelaide Emma aged 4. He also had an older brother aged 18, Joseph Arthur, who was known to his family and friends as Arthur. Both brothers were working as colliers at Aldwarke Main prior to the war. Colliers were welcomed by the military authorities and many signed up as 'pals'. Perhaps John came into Rotherham with other colliers to enlist and he might have signed up with them as a prank. There is absolutely no evidence of this in his service records, but given his impetuous nature it is highly probable that might have happened.

CENSUS OF ENG

Before writing on this Schedule please read the Examples and the Instructions given on the

The contents of the Schedule will be treated as confidential. Strict care will be taken that no information is disclosed with reg

than the pre

NAME AND SURNAME	RELATIONSHIP to Head of Family.	AGE (last Birthday) and SEX.		PARTICULARS as to MARRIAGE.					
of every Person, whether Member of Family, Visitor, Boarder, or Servant, who (1) passed the night of Sunday, April 2nd, 1911, in this dwelling and was alive at midnight, or (2) arrived in this dwelling on the morning of Monday, April 3rd, not having been enumerated elsewhere. No one else must be included. (For order of entering names see Examples on back of Schedule.)	State whether "Head," or "Wife," "Son," "Daughter," or other Relative, "Visitor," "Boarder," or "Servant."	For Infants under one year state the age in months as "under one month," "one month," etc. Ages of Males.	Ages of Females.	Write "Single," "Married," "Widower," or "Widow," opposite the names of all persons aged 15 years and upwards.	Completed years the present Marriage has lasted. If less than one year write "under one."	State, for each Married Woman entered on this Schedule, the number of :— Children born alive to present Marriage. (If no children born alive write "None" in Column 7). Total Children Born Alive.	Children still Living.	Children who have Died.	The reply Professi If engaged particular made or be clearly (See Instruct of Schedu
1.	2.	3.	4.	5.	6.	7.	8.	9.	
1 George Beverley	Head	35		Married 16					Colliery
2 Adelaide Elizabeth Beverley	wife		34	Married	16	4	4	0	
3 Joseph Arthur Beverley	Son	15		—					Colliery
4 John Henry Beverley	Son	13		—					
5 Mary Elizabeth Beverley	Daughter		10	—					
6 Adelaide Emma Beverley	Daughter		7months	—					
7 Wilfred Shaw	Nephew	6		—					—
8									
9									
10									
11									
12									
13									
14									
15									

(To be filled up by the Enumerator.)

I certify that :—
(1.) All the ages on this Schedule are entered in the proper sex columns.
(2.) I have counted the males and females in Columns 3 and 4 separately, and have compared their sum with the total number of persons.
(3.) After making the necessary enquiries I have completed all entries on the Schedule which appeared to be defective, and have corrected such as appeared to be erroneous.

Initials of Enumerator_____

	Total.		
Males.	Females.	Persons.	
4	3	7	

1911 Census return registering that John Henry Beverley was 13 years of age

AND WALES, 1911.

paper, as well as the headings of the Columns. The entries should be written in Ink,

persons. The returns are not to be used for proof of age, as in connection with Old Age Pensions, or for any other purpose
...tical Tables.

Number of Schedule **33**
(To be filled up by the Enumerator after collection.)

PROFESSION or OCCUPATION of Persons aged ten years and upwards.		Whether Employer, Worker, or Working on Own Account.	Whether Working at Home.	BIRTHPLACE of every person.	NATIONALITY of every Person born in a Foreign Country.	INFIRMITY.
	Industry or Service with which worker is connected.	12.	13.	14.	15.	16.
Under Ground	—	Worker	—	Yorks Rotherham	037	—
			—	Yorks Rotherham		
Under Ground		Worker	—	Yorks Rotherham		
		—	—	Yorks Rotherham		
			—	Yorks Rotherham	037	
			—	Yorks Rawmarsh		
			—	Yorks Rotherham	037	

(...be filled up by, or on behalf of, the Head of Family or other person in occupation, or in charge, of this dwelling.)

Number of Rooms in this... Tenement, or Apartment)... as a room but do not count..., lobby, closet, bathroom; ...ffice, shop. **5. 6**

I declare that this Schedule is correctly filled up to the best of my knowledge and belief.

Signature _George Beverley_
Postal Address _66 Park St, Rawmarsh Nr Rotherham yorkshire_

A very youthful looking
John Henry Beverley

What John's service records do reveal, however, is that by 5 September 1914, he was having a medical at Pontefract, where it was recorded that he was almost 5 feet 5 inches tall and weighed 130lb. He was described as having 'grey eyes, darkish brown hair and deemed fit for service'. John was sent to train at Frensham Camp, in Surrey, where he was inoculated against typhoid on 15 October 1914. As part of the training many of the soldiers chose to specialise and John elected to be a bomb-thrower. These bombs were an early form of the more modern grenades, which at the time were known as jam tins by the lads in the regiment and were literally tins filled with dynamite, packed round with stones, to make the most impact. Even later trench bombs were developed with a stick to aid the throwing motion Ann Mapplebeck recalls that on one occasion John had told his mother that the fuses on the bombs were designed to go off after either five or ten seconds. If a bomb-thrower fired his weapon too early, the German soldiers were in the habit of throwing them back into the British lines. The post of bomb-thrower was a dangerous role that was fraught with danger, as many men died during training and never lived to see France at all. Thankfully John was one of the lucky ones who survived training and embarked for France from Southampton on 26 August 1915.

On 9 November 1914, probably not to be outdone by his younger brother, Arthur Beverley also enlisted in Rotherham as a signaller in the East Yorkshire Regiment and he had his medical at Attercliffe, Sheffield, the same day. According to his service records Arthur was aged 19 years and 15 days when he enlisted, which when compared

Great War throwing-bombs excavated at Ypres

with the 1911 census appears to be his true age. His photo indicates a more sober man than his impetuous brother. The family resemblance is seen in his strong slightly prominent nose. His medical records show that he was almost 5 feet 6 inches tall, his weight was 119lb and he was described as having a 'fresh complexion, with hazel eyes and light brown hair'. After his medical, Arthur too received his inoculations, which would render him 'fit for foreign service'.

John's misdemeanours were never very serious, as can be seen by his conduct records, which were usually a few days confined to barracks (CB). Possibly because of his skill as a bomb-thrower, he might have been given light punishments. John's first misdemeanour was understandably for overstaying his first Christmas pass, when he came home to Rotherham to be with his family. The military authorities made no such allowances and with their meticulous recording stated that John was listed as overstaying his pass from 10pm on 23 December 1914 until he returned on 27 December 1914 at 2.15am, for which he served six days CB and forfeited four days leave. His family record that from this point on John was usually reluctant to return to his regiment and

Joseph Arthur Beverley

often went missing. He would have had no illusions about the conditions at the Front, but he still returned to do his duty. John was once again confined to barracks on 23 May 1915, simply for being 'absent from church parade' at 8.45am. His older brother Arthur's records indicate that he was slightly less rebellious than his brother and his conduct sheet states that he was only charged with a) not complying with an order, and b) using obscene language to an NCO, for which he received seven days CB on 21 June 1915. Whilst in France serving as a signaller Arthur had not forgotten his little sister Adelaide, and he sent her a card writing 'From your loving brother, Arthur' and sending her 'love and kisses'.

On 9 July 1916 John Beverley's medical records show he was wounded by gunshot to his left arm, his left side and his right leg. As a result of these injuries he was sent back to England to a military hospital to recover. He was discharged on 10 October, where he quickly

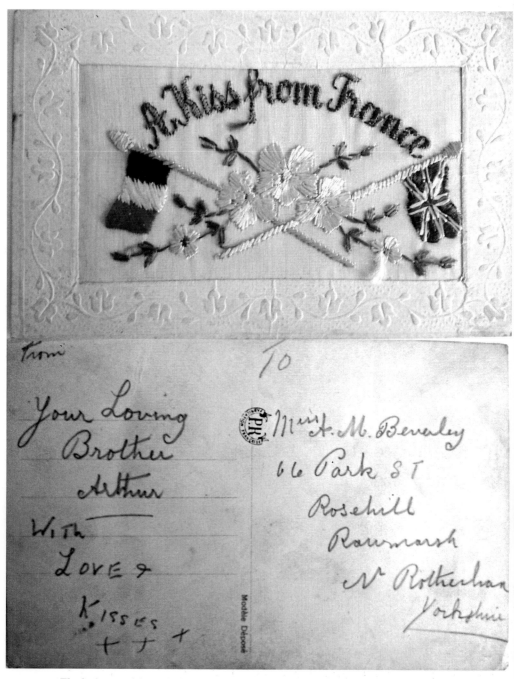

The loving card from Arthur Beverley sent to his sister Adelaide

rejoined his regiment. The following year John overstayed Christmas leave again by three days in January 1917, for which he got five days CB. Once again the meticulous recording by the military authorities show that he extended his leave without permission by two days, five hours and twenty minutes. On 1 June he was in Sunderland seeing an eye specialist and was in hospital there, although the service records give no hint of what the problem was. Meanwhile, his brother, Arthur, received a certificate in June 1917 recording his 'distinguished conduct on the field of battle'. The notation from the major general of his Unit, David M Campbell, states:

> Your commanding officer and brigade commander have informed me that you distinguished yourself in the field on 1st & 17th July and 16th & 25th September 1916. I congratulate you on your fine work.

On 25 June 1917, John too was charged with a) refusing to obey an order, and b) using obscene and threatening language, and his punishment was ten days CB. Later the following month he continued to absent himself without leave, whilst he was still convalescing in Sunderland. On that occasion he was arrested by the Military Police

The card from his Major General David M. Campbell congratulating Arthur Beverley on his distinguished conduct

TWENTY-FIRST DIVISION

BRITISH EXPEDITIONARY FORCE

No. 14864 Pte. g a. Beverley

1 East Yorks R.

Your Commanding Officer and Brigade Commander have informed me that you distinguished yourself in the Field on the 1st – 17th July & 16th – 25th Sept. 1916.

I congratulate you on your fine work.

David M Campbell

MAJOR-GENERAL,
Commanding 21st Division.

Royal Humane Society
INSTITUTED 1774.

INCORPORATED BY ROYAL CHARTER

PATRON,

His Majesty the King

VICE PRESIDENT,

The Most Hon. the Marquis of Breadalbane, K.G.

At a Meeting of the Committee of the Royal Humane Society
held at 4, Trafalgar Square, Charing Cross
on the 9th day of October 1917

Present   Admiral Sir G. Digby Morant, K.C.B.   in the Chair

It was Resolved Unanimously that

Pte. J. Beverley

is justly entitled to the Honorary Testimonial of this Society inscribed on
Vellum which is hereby awarded him for having on the 4th September
1917 gone to the rescue of a boy who was in imminent danger of drowning
in the sea at Sunderland and whose life he gallantly saved.

Breadalbane
Vice President.

F. A. C. Claughton
Secretary.

G. Digby Morant
Chairman.

John Beverley's Certificate from the Humane Society, dated October 1917

on Coronation Street, Sunderland, at quarter to twelve on 27 August 1917, for which he served four days CB.

Yet the bravery of John Beverley was never in doubt, as was proved on 4 September 1917 when he and a colleague, Corporal Price, saved a boy from drowning at the Boat House Guard, Sunderland. For this action he was awarded the Humane Society Certificate the following month. The certificate notes that the two men had 'gone to the rescue of a boy who was in imminent danger of drowning in the sea at Sunderland, and whose life they gallantly saved'. The *Rotherham Express* of 24 November 1917 recorded the award, stating that Mrs Beverley had received the following letter:

> *The General Officer commanding the section of the York and Lancaster declares that on the part of Corporal Price and Private Beverley, who on the 4th September at great risk to themselves, saved a boy from drowning at the Boat House Guard, Sunderland. The gallantry and promptitude displayed by them is worthy of the greatest praise'.*

The newspaper also records that Private Beverley continued to recover from his wounds, and his mother received a letter stating that he was 'getting along fine'.

There is little doubt that Mr and Mrs Beverley, like many Rotherham parents at the time, were extremely proud of their two gallant sons, but unfortunately all that was about to come to an end. By October 1917 it was reported that their oldest son, Arthur, had been shot and killed on the 4th. The *Advertiser* praised the soldier 'who had fought in most of the theatres of war, receiving wounds at Mons and Neuve Chapelle and had also been involved in the battles on the Somme and on Vimy Ridge'. It was reported that he had been killed in action whilst 'saving the life of an officer', and had died four days later at 'a casualty clearing station in France'. His parents received a letter from his commanding officer who told of his bravery:

> *It is extremely painful for me to have to tell you that your son Private J. A. Beverley has died of wounds. He went into action with us, and was wounded on the fourth instant in the arm, thigh and abdomen. I got him away as quickly as possible down to the dressing station, and got a message yesterday to say that he had*

*died. He was a very gallant and brave fellow and always ready
to do any sort of job, no matter how dangerous. He was one of
my best men in signal section and very hard working. Even under
the most trying circumstances he was always the most cheerful.
His death is a great loss to me, and the signallers all desire me to
express their deepest sympathy to you in your terrible loss, to
which I should like to add my own.*

So popular was Arthur with the East Yorkshire Regiment that his
parents also received a letter from the chaplain of the unit and others
from some of his comrades. It is to be hoped that this was of some
comfort to Mr and Mrs Beverley. They were later notified that his body
was buried in the British Cemetery at Godewaersvelde, about 4¾miles
from Poperinghe. The following year a letter was sent to Mrs Beverley
dated 7 February 1918 from an unnamed officer at the Infantry Record
Office, York. The letter included some articles belonging to Arthur,
which were to be returned to his parents. The articles consisted of
various photos, two discs, a wallet, a matchbox case, a testament and
a cotton bag. Mrs Beverley sent the receipt dated 12 February to
acknowledge the few articles. At the same time she was told that she
would receive a small pension but that would not have been sufficient
compensation for the loss of her oldest son.

It was while he was still in Sunderland that John heard about his
brother's death. It might have been some reaction to the news when he
received his last recorded offence on 8 November 1917. It was for
being a mere twenty minutes late while on active service, for which he
served three days CB. Later that month the regiment was sent to Italy,
but John was fighting in France by 21 March 1918, when he too was
sadly killed. He died on the very first day of the massive attacks all
along the Western Front known as the Ludendorff Offensive. The
Germans, who knew that the United States would soon be involved in
the war, threw everything they had at the British and Allied troops. The
war diary reports that 'the support line was heavily shelled' and as a
consequence John was one of eight soldiers who died in the fighting
that day.[14] Unfortunately this very brave Rotherham lad is one of the
many millions who has no known grave as their bodies were never
found. However Private John Henry Beverley's name is remembered
with others at the Faubourg – D'Amiens Cemetery in France. Like

many parents in the town of Rotherham, Mr and Mrs Beverley had lost both sons to the war. It was said that Mrs Beverley never got over the death of her two sons, and was unable to care for her youngest daughter, Adelaide Emma, aged 4, who was sent to live with relatives in Wales. Ann Mapplebeck also said that such was Mrs Beverley's grief that she went grey overnight.

Despite news from both official and unofficial channels, many families in Rotherham remained ignorant of the way their relatives had died. After a battle many soldiers who had been killed were buried where they fell. One such was Corporal J. Wright, a machine-gunner of Duncan Street, Canklow, whose death was reported in November 1917. The news was particularly hard as his mother, Mrs Wright, had suffered the loss of her husband only the year before in an accident at Rotherham Main Colliery where he worked. It is to be hoped that the details of the death of her son was of some consolation to Mrs Wright. His commanding officer wrote:

Please accept the sincere sympathy of myself and the men of the 148th Machine Gun Company in the great loss you have sustained in the death of your son. He has been under my command in both the B and D sections since last January, and I cannot speak too highly of him, both as a gallant soldier and a good comrade. We

Corporal J. Wright's name on the War Memorial in Clifton Park

of the old company, who are left, feel the loss of your boy very much. He was killed instantly and suffered no pain, which I am sure will be at least a great comfort for you to know. We buried him on the battlefield where he fell, which I think is the most fitting resting place for such a gallant fellow'.

His name was later inscribed in the Great War Memorial in Clifton Park.

These are the stories of just a few of the gallant men who left Rotherham to fight for king and country, leaving behind relatives who waited anxiously for news. The letters of Samuel Maiden and the service records of John and Arthur Beverley show they were just ordinary men doing their duty, in the hope that one day they would return to the town of their birth.

CHAPTER 5

Anti-German feeling in Rotherham

Almost as soon as war was declared, local and national newspapers were reporting atrocities committed by 'the German Hun'. In Rotherham, as in many other towns of Britain, there were a number of German civilians who had lived peacefully in the town up to the outbreak of war. Overnight they found that they were viewed with suspicion by neighbours and former friends. Once war had been declared, the Rotherham police force had been informed by telegram from the War Office that:

> *All German men of fighting age were to present themselves to the police authorities. All cases of such men were in turn to be reported to the nearest military authorities, who would take the appropriate action'*

In Rotherham the German civilians readily complied with the order and within a few days several registered as aliens at the different police stations throughout the district. Even though they had lived in the area for many years, they still had to 'demonstrate a good character and a good knowledge of the English language'. Some were recognised to be outstanding citizens, such as Alderman Frederick Schonhut. He had lived in Rotherham for more than forty years and was held in such high esteem that he was elected onto the town council. Another member of his family, Frederick Charles Schonhut, also took over the management of the Red Lion Hotel in the town centre. At the outbreak of war a rumour went around the town that Frederick Charles had expressed hostility to England and that he destroyed a picture of King George and replaced it with one of the kaiser. Such was the outrage of this man who was a British subject that he took an advert in the *Rotherham Advertiser* dated 8 August 1914 to deny such slander and to offer a substantial reward for the names and addresses of persons spreading or repeating such lies.

By September 1914, Inspector Green of Rotherham Police admitted to the Revision Court that there were nineteen German aliens scattered throughout the district. He told the court that when they had first come to Rotherham and taken up a trade in the town, ten had been put onto the register of voters as a matter of course because of their employment. However, since war had been declared all rights of citizenship had been revoked and they were now no longer able to vote. The inspector stated to the members of the court, that all the Rotherham German aliens had already registered with the police and that they had obeyed the law in every way. The *Advertiser*, dated 19 September 1914, referred to the ten voters and confidently stated that:

> *It would seem therefore that Rotherham had nothing to fear from the aliens within her gates, all of whom are willing and anxious to live at peace with our people [...] and we have been spared any of the unwarranted displays of feeling which other towns have had to deplore. The ten aliens who have been struck off the register, will of course come back to the enjoyment of full citizenship when peace is once more reached'.*

Nevertheless, their freedom was constricted. On 6 August 1914, the military authorities announced that all German aliens were to be made prisoners-of-war and interned. They were also forbidden to possess or drive a vehicle without the written permission of the police authorities. In a secret memo police officers were requested to keep a close watch for aliens who 'might be travelling in motor vehicles to commit outrages'. This ban on vehicles meant that many Germans lost their employment. Indeed so much suspicion was cast on them, that on 26 September 1914 it was announced that a workmen at Moorgate Cemetery was a German, and despite being a good worker he had been asked to leave.

Name: **Harry Abel**

Born: 30th April 1884

Place of Birth: **Rotherham**

Born to: (Father): **Frederick Abel**

       (Mother): **Sophia Abel (nee Loo)**

Married: **Jane Whelan**

Died: 1st December 1965 aged 81

Picture of Harry Abel giving names of his mother and father, and the date of his death

The lead-up to the national anti-German feeling towards people of German descent had begun in October 1914 in Parliament, when Lord Charles Beresford urged his fellow countrymen to take a strong line of action with regard to 'the crowds of alien enemies in our midst'. It was not long before Rotherham people were writing anonymous letters about their former countrymen. One such letter, addressed to the editor of the *Advertiser* and signed 'from a Britisher', was printed on 17 October. The letter drew the attention of the reader to the 'large numbers of Germans in our town and neighbourhood' and stated that:

Doubtless they are naturalised or of naturalised German parentage, but all the same their sympathies must lie with the enemy. I think as loyal Britons we should refuse to trade with these people, and purchase from English people only. I was much struck on Saturday night last, by large crowds who were doing business at shops with German names over the doors.

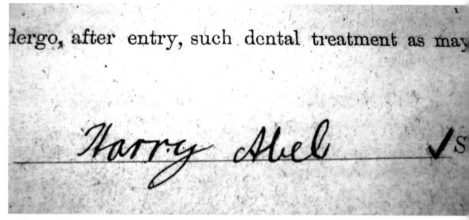

Harry Abel's signature when he transferred to Royal Naval Division as part of the
Collingwood Battalion in September 1914

The following week another letter with the title *The Enemy in Our Midst* agreed, that:

> *Facts are daily coming to light, showing in a most astonishing manner the extent of the German espionage system. Germans, who we thought to be friends, are proved to be spies.*

The writer stated that these men should 'be moved to a place of security' and there was no place for 'flabby sentimentality'. This letter too was signed 'Another Britisher'.

Some Germans tried to enlist, but many were turned away at the recruitment office where they were seen as spies. Thankfully, those with more English sounding names were more successful. One Rotherham man who managed to enlist was Harry Abel, a collier who had been born in Rotherham in April 1884. He was registered as a British subject, although his parents, Frederick and Sophia, had been born at Wurttemberg, Germany. The family are unsure exactly when Harry's parents came to Rotherham, but relative Kathleen Senior found them in the 1871 census living at Midland Road, Masbrough. Fortunately, Harry's parents died before they could see the hostility that took over the town of Rotherham. Frederick died in Rotherham in March 1908, aged 64, and his wife died in February 1910. When war broke out, Harry was living at a house on Greasbrough Road,

Rotherham, with his wife Jane and their five children. The photograph that remains of Harry shows a determined man intent on doing his patriotic duty for the country of his birth. The children, two boys and three girls, were given very English names of Harry, Hilda, Elizabeth, Florence and Thomas. Up to the outbreak of war their father had always been considered by others to be a respectable member of the community, described as a fair-minded man who would often intervene with local domestic disputes in the area where he lived. Harry certainly showed no hesitation in enlisting and he joined the York and Lancaster Regiment on 31 August 1914. Just a week later he was transferred to Royal Naval Division as part of the Collingwood Battalion. His signature on the papers agreeing to the transfer indicate a firm and confident hand. Harry's service papers reveal that he was 5' 11" tall, aged 30 years and 4 months, and was described as having brown eyes and hair and weighing 156lb. He was given a medical examination at Rotherham on the date of enlistment where he was deemed 'fit to enlist'.

On 3 October, his division were given orders that they were moving to Antwerp and three days later they were in action, but the fighting was hard. Five days later orders were issued for the battalion to retire and Harry was one of the many men captured that day. His family were told on 29 November 1914 that he had been reported missing. It was some months before they learned he had been made a prisoner-of-war. Harry spent the rest of the war interned at Doeberitz in Germany. There is little doubt that his German ancestry gained him no special treatment in the camp. Harry Abel, like millions of other men, refused to talk about the war when he came back to Rotherham, but to the end of his days he kept an album of photographs from that time. Frustratingly the albums are full of pictures of other unnamed prisoners. Harry was finally repatriated back to this country on 30 December 1918, when he landed at Hull. Like other ex-prisoners-of-war he was glad to be back in Rotherham, although when he returned he was shocked to hear about the hostility shown to his wife and children while he was away.

For a while the antagonism of the people of the town against the Germans in their midst appeared to be fading, but this was all to change following the sinking of the *Lusitania* on the afternoon of Friday 7 May 1915. The boat, which had been carrying civilians, was torpedoed and

Picture of some unnamed prisoners in Harry Abel's prisoner-of-war photograph album

sunk by a German U-boat shortly after leaving Liverpool. A Rotherham man, Mr Ernest Drakeford, was among the survivors and he wrote immediately to his parents at Bridge Street, Swinton, to let them know he was safe and well. He described how, after he finished work at 2am, the men heard a loud thud and noted that the ship began to list. Ernest described how people were rushing about in the dark on the decks, and said that the cries of the women and children were pitiful to hear. He and Mr Crank, the 31-year-old baggage master, helped each other to put on their life jackets. He described how in the panic:

One of the boats were being lowered full of people, among whom there was a great number of women and children. The rope at one end gave way, the boat plunging down into the water, emptying out most of the people. Then to try to save the situation someone

cut the other end of the rope and the boat crashed down on the
people underneath, and they must have been killed, injured or
drowned.

Ernest knew that the *Lusitania* was going to sink, so he slid down the deck and jumped into the sea, quickly followed by all the objects that had been on the deck. He managed to get to the surface just in time to see the great ship's funnels go under the water. Ernest told his parents that he saw people climbing onto any wreckage they could find and the shouts and cries for help filled the air. Luckily he found a water barrel and hung onto it for dear life. All the time he was in the water he had to keep pushing wreckage and bodies away for fear of being dragged under or crushed. Ernest called out to a passing boat to save him, but he could see it was full already. Finally he saw the ship's boatswain in a collapsible boat, and he shouted out. The boatswain saw him and told him to stay where he was, and he would come soon and pick him up. After the boatswain had helped a couple of women on board, they picked up Ernest and lay him down in the boat. Eventually they were rescued by a steamer and given tea and biscuits. Thankfully, Ernest arrived in Rotherham on Sunday 9 May 1915 at 7am.

Throughout Britain, the anger of the people turned against Germany at the news of the sinking of the *Lusitania*. As an indication of the outrage felt by this one act, an unnamed Rotherham corporal attached to the Black Watch Regiment, wrote home to his parents to tell them that his regiment had a new battle cry. As men went into combat, shouts of 'remember the *Lusitania*' were heard. He said it transformed the men from the 'previously kind-hearted soldiers, into an avenging fury'. The rabid anti-German feeling that was now sweeping all over the country must have badly shaken the German men and women living in Rotherham. On Thursday 13 May 1915, a deputation made an impassioned application to the mayor, Alderman P. Bancroft Coward. They handed him a declaration at his chambers at the town hall that stated:

We the undersigned, after being resident in Rotherham for some
40 years and over, have always been loyal subjects to the king
and country, though of South German birth. We hereby enter our
strongest protest against the barbaric conduct which has been

practised, and the methods adopted by the kaiser and his Prussians in waging war against non combatants, and especially against innocent women and children. We look upon the sinking of the Lusitania with the gravest horror, and we wish to record most emphatically our great indignation at the crimes which have been committed'.

But if they hoped that this declaration would save them they were very wrong. News filtered into the town on Friday 14 May 1915 that even in the usually quiet districts of Mexborough, Conisborough and Denaby, German families had been attacked and shops and premises smashed by angry neighbours. That same night the riots started in Rotherham at the site of Messrs Leonard Fishers, a pork butcher's shop on St Ann's Road. It was reported that the premises were so looted that 'it was not long before little that was thought worth taking away, was left'. The rioters then moved on to Hannemann's butcher's on Frederick Street, where half-bricks were thrown at the windows. Once again, not content with just taking merchandise out of the windows, the house behind was broken into and domestic goods removed. So bad was the damage that it was later reported that only the kitchen table was left intact.

Someone in the crowd mentioned that there was a member of the Schonhut family who had taken over the Red Lion Hotel, and the crowd swerved off in that direction. Due to the quick decision made by the police, the rioters found the yard gates of the hotel closed against them. Nevertheless, they made sure that all the windows overlooking Bridgegate were smashed. Later that same night the premises of Karl Wagelein of Bridgegate, another pork butcher, was attacked and broken into. Similarly, the windows of Mr C. Kheeler of Ferham Road were smashed and goods removed. Then the crowd moved to the premises rented by Mr Frederick Schonhut on Masbrough Street before heading to Mr E. C. Schonhut's butcher's shop on Doncastergate. However, the crowd were in for disappointment as the shutters had been put up and the family had wisely gone out of town.

The mob, which now numbered in thousands, collected at the crossroads of Doncastergate, Wellgate, High Street and College Street. At this point the police realised that they were heavily outnumbered and consequently had great difficulty in restraining the crowd. Officers

All the windows of the Red Lion Hotel overlooking Bridgegate were smashed in the anti German riots in Rotherham in May 1915

were forced to watch powerlessly as the shutters of the Schonhut's butchers shop on Doncastergate were torn down and the windows smashed. Soon the looters were removing stock before they attacked the shop owned by Mr Harry Carley on Wellgate. Once again his windows were broken and items removed, and domestic objects from the house were thrown into the street. Afterwards it was reported that people were seen walking away along Westgate, with the chairs that had belonged to Mr Carley. Another property belonging to Mr J. W. Limbach of Bridgegate was also attacked before the crowd tried to return, unsuccessfully, to the Red Lion Hotel. Gradually the police gained control and the crowd was finally dispersed. Despite the wreckage of the shops, thankfully there was only one fatality, a little boy who was knocked down by a lorry. Sadly the child died before reaching hospital.

In the morning the evidence of the night's looting was still to be seen. The gates to the yard of the Red Lion were barred and shuttered and large placards had been pinned to them. These informed the people of the town that Frederick Schonhut had been relieved as the manager of the hotel. The owners, Messrs Tennants of Sheffield, announced that

Bridgegate today – in May 1914 five mounted police horses dashed down Bridgegate in an attempt to scatter the crowd intent on looting the Red Lion Hotel

they had a new manager and reminded people that many of their employees 'were serving with the colours'. The placards appealed to people to protect the property from further attack. But members of the Rotherham police force were more prepared on the Saturday and had drafted in extra officers from other nearby towns. Nevertheless, a large crowd returned that evening once again to attack the Red Lion Hotel. It seemed that the building had become a focus for the feelings of hatred against German people. As the numbers in the crowd grew, cries of 'down with the kaiser' and 'down with the Germans' were heard from the angry mob. A force of twenty-four police constables guarded the gates of the hotel when a loud hooting was heard and down Bridgegate galloped five mounted police horses. Missiles of all descriptions were thrown at the horses but it was past midnight before order was restored.

The repercussions of the rioting, however, continued to be felt for weeks afterwards. Several people were arrested and fined for looting and inciting the crowd to riot. On Thursday 20 May a hasty application was heard in the Borough Court requesting that the licence of the Red Lion Hotel be transferred from Mr F. C. Schonhut to Mr Ben Smith, who had been the previous manager of the Belvedere Hotel on Moorgate. The application was swiftly agreed by the magistrates. It seems that the Rotherham riots had been quashed, but the previously respectable shopkeepers of German descent had their shops and homes attacked and their possessions stolen. It was rumoured that one family, which included young children, had been attacked and not only lost their home but even the baby clothes had been plundered. For many weeks German families were left homeless and the families destitute, and were forced to apply to the Rotherham Guardians for workhouse relief. The *Rotherham Advertiser*, trying to explain the riot, concluded in the familiar propagandist-speak of the time that referred to the German people as baby killers:

Rotherham people are not Huns. They bear no enmity, unless it is deserved, and they are ever ready to assist helpless people. They smashed the shops of German people as a protest against the inhumanity of the German authorities; but they can well afford to leave the baby killers to the tender mercies of our soldiers and sailors, who have sworn to make them squirm for all their atrocities. And they will do it.

So ended an episode of which Rotherham people must look back on with shame. But that was no consolation for those German people who saw themselves as true 'Rotherhamites' and who had lived in the town peaceably for many years prior to the sinking of the *Lusitania*.

CHAPTER 6

Modern technology

At the beginning of the Great War the army relied very heavily on cavalry units. One of the first demands that the military authorities made after enlistment in Rotherham was to collect or commandeer horses that could be used in the war. Recruitment of men to care for horses also took place in November 1915. This new battalion was to be called the Forage Department Army Service Corps. Later in the war a Women's Forage Corps was introduced. Both were recruited to care for the army horses.

In a letter that arrived in Rotherham on 2 September 1914, Corporal John Bottom of the 18th Royal Hussars spoke about the difficulties of working with horses. He complains to his father, Mr Frank Bottom of James Street, Masbrough, that he was saddle sore. Even as he was in the middle of writing the letter, he said that he would have to close now, as the men had once again got their orders to saddle up and move. These orders were usually transmitted to the men by the use of bugle calls requesting them to saddle up. The vulnerability of these brave animals was described as Corporal Bottom proudly told his father that he had three horses shot out from under him. He stated that although he had been slightly wounded on one occasion, he had quickly gone back to the front after only ten days rest. Corporal Bottom ended his letter with a prayer familiar to most people serving at the Front. 'I hope and pray that God will see me home safe again.' Unfortunately this brave soldier was killed in action on 13 May 1915, aged only 23. His death was described by a comrade, Private J. R. Seaton, who was with

A bugle dating from the Great War

him in the trenches just outside Ypres. His letter to Private Bottom's parents stated that the offensive had started on that morning just before dawn. When the Germans sent over their first shell, that was the signal for one of the biggest bombardments that the whole battalion had witnessed in the campaign. Private Seaton said:

> *The last time I saw John was about 4am in the morning and he was quite alright then, but I heard later that he had been killed by a piece of shell, whilst helping to dig some more men out from under this great fall of earth [...] I was wounded before the fighting was over, but I can tell this, poor 'Jack' as we called him was killed instantly, so he didn't suffer and no soldier died more nobly [...] helping to dig out some that were buried alive.*

Private Seaton hoped that the information that his friend had died bravely and had been buried would have been of some consolation to his family. Private John Bottom's name is inscribed on the Rotherham cenotaph and on a memorial headstone in Kimberworth churchyard. Only as the new technology of weaponry developed did the military authorities recognise the vulnerability of the horse and its rider, and gradually horses were replaced by more sophisticated weaponry.

Private J. Bottom's name on the Cenotaph in Clifton Park, Rotherham

In June 1915 Rotherham was asked to develop its very own Howitzer Brigade, which had cannons capable of firing shells at a very high trajectory, causing maximum damage to the enemy. The recruitment in the town was swift and on 5 July over 4,000 new troops assembled in Clifton Park for an inspection by Major General Sir J. K. Trotter. The inspection was a great success, but little did the proud members of the new brigade realise that they would soon be involved in a national scandal. The following month training was held in the park and it was not long before the Rotherham Parks Committee was complaining that members of the brigade had damaged flowerbeds and trees with the gun carriage. It was reported in a town council meeting that two benches had also been damaged by the carriage and the bark had been stripped from five young poplar trees by horses that had been tethered there. The unpatriotic comments made by the committee were quickly picked up and repeated by the national press. Consequently, the *Advertiser* stated that the Parks Committee had:

> *[...] held Rotherham up to the ridicule of the whole country, which should cause the people of the town to hang their heads in shame and disgust, that it should have reached the ears of the brave Rotherham sons who are risking everything on the front line.*

But if the Rotherham authorities hoped that the matter would swiftly become yesterday's news they were in for a shock. By this time local newspapers were being widely distributed to the men fighting in France, sent by their relatives. Consequently, on 21 August 1915 a parcel was delivered to the editor of the *Rotherham Advertiser* marked 'with care'. The parcel had come from France and upon opening it very carefully the staff found some pieces of bark that were enclosed. A note explained:

> *We are sending you this piece of bark originally forming part of the exterior of a fine old tree in a magnificent private park here in Northern France, but which had the misfortune to lose its beauty through getting in the way of German shells. We are sending it to you so that you might, if you think fit, publicly present it to the Rotherham Parks Committee, to make good the loss sustained when the horses belonging to the Rotherham Howitzer Brigade had the impudence to chew the bark off a tree in Clifton Park [...] Rotherham seems to think more of its trees than it does of the lives of soldiers who are helping to protect it.*

The embarrassing matter was brought up by the town council again on 9 October 1915, when the Parks Committee was forced to apologise. The council minutes note that 'every member of the council felt that no affront was intended to the brave soldiers of the town' and promised that 'the offending minutes would be expunged from the record'. It was hoped that this would bring an end to the matter. The Rotherham Howitzer Brigade went on to win many military honours and the Howitzer guns themselves became more sophisticated and were used extensively in World War Two.

But the one new innovation that inspired fear in most British people was the development of the zeppelins. It is possible that Germany had no intention of aerial bombardment when they built the large rigid airships named after their maker, Count Ferdinand von Zeppelin. They were used commercially in 1910 and initially seen as a form of luxury travel. However, following the outbreak of hostilities, these airships were seen as being useful for spying on the enemy and taking photographs behind British and Allied lines in order to gather information. Very soon it was decided they could be used to drop bombs. Certainly in England the fear of invasion became more real when it was reported that these airships could carry up to twenty-five men and twelve tons of explosives. Whatever the German's original intention, it was not long before bombing raids took place over Britain's east coast by zeppelins in 1916.

As early as 26 August 1914, the danger of attack from the air had been noted in Rotherham, when the police inspectors notebook contained a request that all officers take note:

The kind of bombs that Germans threw from the zeppelins

Any aeroplane, balloon or flying machine should be reported to police headquarters without delay, and that the officer will take particular notice of the direction in which it is flying.

These fears were realised on Monday 25 September 1916 when two zeppelins, no doubt looking for the industrial areas of Sheffield and Rotherham, were seen. The people of Rotherham had been informed of what precautionary measures to take, in the instance of hostile aircraft raids as early as February 1915. They were that:

All inhabitants and passengers in the streets should at once take refuge. The safest places are cellars or the lowest room in each building.

When the zeppelins were first spotted a buzzer was sounded and soon the people of the town heard the engines. Despite strict instructions to shelter in cellars and indoors, hundreds of Rotherham people went out into the fields to see these monsters for themselves. It was later reported that many of these men and women carried children in their arms. Shortly after midnight several witnesses described how:

Flashes of fire resembling lightning, illuminated the sky and these were followed in rapid succession by loud reports of exploding bombs. Many such reports were counted. No damage whatever in the town itself was done,

The inside of a typical German bomb

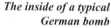

Houses on St Ann's Road today, just below the church

and no personal injuries were sustained. What is more there was no panic among the people.

A beam from a searchlight tried to pick out the raiders in the sky, but they could not be clearly seen, as it was such a cloudy night. The whole raid was over in about ten or fifteen minutes, and the following morning evidence of the bombs were found. Although about twenty bombs had been dropped, several had not gone off and these were closely guarded by the police. Sadly on this visit by zeppelins, although no inhabitants of Rotherham were seriously injured, several people were killed in Sheffield as they slept in their beds.

The military authorities were aware from the outset that enemy aircraft could be attracted to the town by lights on the ground. Instructions were issued under the Defence of the Realm Act (known as DORA) on 5 February 1915, restricting the lights of motor cars, streetlamps and tramcars. But it was the concern that lighting from houses would attract bombing that permeated throughout the police force notebooks in the years of the Great War. A complaint was made on 7 August 1915 of a house on St Ann's Road situated 'just below St Stephen's Church where a skylight had been brightly lit at night time. Ten days later, attention was drawn to the same offence from a house at either number 7 or 9 Lindum Terrace. In both cases officers were alerted to keep a strict watch. The police inspectors book records that on 16 September 1916 a confidential note had been received from the military authorities informing Mr Weatherhogg that 'the lighting regulations were not being strictly adhered to in Rotherham'. The problem continued throughout the years of the Great War, despite the regular inspections and letters to householders.

Rotherham had several anti-aircraft guns strategically placed, so there was a very real chance that a German zeppelin could be brought down over the town, and on 28 March 1918 instructions were issued about what to do in such an event. The Rotherham chief constable issued orders to his men that the crew of enemy aircraft should be removed from the wreckage as quickly as possible. They should then be:

Houses on Lindum Terrace as it is today

[…] scrupulously searched for any papers etc. Any attempt on their part to destroy papers or the aircraft should be stopped. No conversation between the prisoner and their guards should take place (unless with a medical officer in case of injury) prior to expert officers questioning them.

As early as May 1912 it was thought that aeroplanes, like the zeppelins, could be useful as a tool of aerial photography, and the Royal Flying Corps was formed. By the beginning of the war there had been many successful flights over enemy lines when photographs of the enemy's position could be taken and studied carefully. In the trenches the sight of an aircraft was becoming more common, but to the people of Rotherham, it was still a rare sight. So it was quite exciting when, in December 1914, an early report about a dogfight that took place in the air over France was printed in the *Advertiser*. Private E. Lawton (the same soldier who had made use of socks as gloves) had described the scene in a letter to his wife at their home on Shakespeare Road. He had been stationed 'somewhere in France' when the men on the ground were treated to a fantastic spectacle. He told his wife that two British and two French biplanes met four German planes and they circled round, each trying to gain an advantage on the enemy. Suddenly the two British and French planes flew away in parallel lines, the Germans in hot pursuit:

> *Then with equal suddenness, a shower of shells burst around the German machines who found they had been led into a trap. Our machines had led them over hidden French batteries and within a few minutes all the four German planes were blown to pieces and the pilots killed.'*

By June of 1917 aircraft were in regular use and the York and Lancaster war diary reports that regular raids were now being carried out over enemy lines with 'aeroplane co-operation'. [17] We certainly know that French and German towns were being bombed and many of the roads were reported as being filled with refugees escaping from the towns. The enemy also realised the better use of the aeroplane as bombers and the war diary records that 'two men were killed and twelve wounded in a hostile air raid over the camp in France, where the men were billeted' on 18 October 1917.

Refugees fleeing the French town of Poperinghe in 1914

Some soldiers, who had quickly recognised the importance of such machines, often transferred from other regiments into the burgeoning Royal Flying Corps. One of the first reports from a missing airman, Lieutenant Charles B. Bird, came to the town in February 1917. His mother, Mrs C. H. Jones of Potter Hill, Greasbrough, had been informed that her son was missing, but ironically had recently received a letter from him. In the letter he told her that he was due some leave and was looking forward to seeing her in a month or so. Like many other pilots of the RFC, Lieutenant Bird at first joined the army and served in India before returning to Britain in 1910 with the rank of bombardier. In 1914 he volunteered to join the Dragoons where he soon received the Military Cross for 'conspicuous gallantry after protracted operations' in August 1916. Soon after being awarded the medal, he joined the RFC before being reported as missing. Thankfully, the following month, his mother received a telegram saying that he had been taken a prisoner and was at a camp in Germany.

The year after, on what was to prove the last of the war, the tragic death of a pilot from Rotherham, Major Leslie Peech Aizlewood was reported. He was the only son of the mayor of the town and had gone to university in Sheffield, where he studied applied science before starting work at the Parkgate Iron and Steelworks. He enlisted as a territorial in the York and Lancaster Regiment in 1912 and on the outbreak of hostilities went to France with the Expeditionary Force, before being invalided home in July 1915. After he recovered, he joined the RFC and a month later was made captain. In March 1916 he went to Buckingham Palace where he received his MC from the king for conspicuous gallantry and skill when:

> *Seeing five hostile machines, he manoeuvred to get between them and their lines. Then diving at one of them, he reserved his fire until he was only 20 yards off. The hostile machine fell out of control, but he was so close that he collided with it, breaking his propeller and damaging his machine. Though it was barely controllable, he managed to get back to his own lines.*

He was appointed to a School of Aerial Fighting at Ayr as chief instructor with the temporary rank of major in October 1917, and promoted to squadron commander on 1 January 1918. The Royal Air Force was created on 1 April 1918 and on 27 April 1918, Leslie was appointed to another training school at Marske, North Yorkshire, as commanding officer. Sadly, it was from there on 29 September 1918 that news came that he had been killed in an accident. His plane, a Sopwith Camel, had plunged into the sea during a training flight, which was being filmed at the time. His body was buried in the church yard of St Germain's at Marske with full military honours. A court of enquiry into the crash found that the elevator controls had become jammed in his flying clothes. Major Aizlewood was awarded the Air Force Cross posthumously on 3 January 1919. Despite his sad death, the effect that these machines made on the town and cities of Britain could not be underestimated. No longer did we see ourselves as an island and warfare would never be the same again.

Massive improvements in warfare were being made, but at the same time the years of the Great War also saw other less technological innovations. One of these was in the manufacture and use of barbed wire. This was mainly strung across No-Man's-Land to create a deadly obstacle to advancing troops. So successful was it that that specially trained men (called sappers) would creep out of the trenches at night in order to repair any damaged wire and also to spoil that of the enemy. Acres of this wire were stretched across metal poles, which could be easily inserted in the ground. By the spring of 1915, barbed wire was

Iron poles through which barbed wire was strung, still at the side of the road at Ypres

an essential component of warfare, whilst on the other hand it caused a great stumbling block for men going over the top.

Perhaps the biggest wartime technological innovation was possibly developed as a reaction to the stalemate of trench warfare when military authorities developed tanks that were at first referred to as land ships. On 2 November 1917, Colonel Wylie records that the York and Lancaster Regiment had 'a special two day course of training with tanks, ready for the battle of Cambrai where it was intended they should

Reels of barbed wire still seen in Ypres

be used'. He recorded 'the steel monsters inspired great confidence in all ranks'.

Despite this these early tanks proved to be cumbersome and unreliable and all too easily bogged down in the mud. An example of this reached Rotherham in November 1917 when a local hero, Captain Donald Hickling Richardson, son of the MP for the town, was awarded the MC for bravery. The incident in which he received the medal occurred when their tank was crossing English lines and the tank commander was wounded. Captain Richardson took over command

and was moving the tank forward when it was ditched. The British infantry surrounding the area were driven back and, as a result, the tank and the men inside it were isolated for two days and nights behind enemy lines. The efficiency of the large machine was vindicated when officers and crew of the tank, even though they were all wounded, survived snipers during the day and attacks on the tank at night. The Germans even got on top of the tank and fired at it with machine-guns, but without any effect. The men inside survived and managed to maintain themselves for fifty-two hours before the ground was regained and they were released by British troops. On Wednesday 6 February 1918, Captain Richardson went to Buckingham Palace, where he was presented with his medal by the king. He was also awarded the Croix de Guerre by the King of the Belgians for his bravery.

Although tanks never made the impact in the Great War as they did in the next war, for the first time in August 1918 the war diary records that 'tanks much in use'.

CHAPTER 7

The RAMC and wounded soldiers

In any war the military authorities have to make provision for wounded men and historically there have always been regimental surgeons attached to each battalion. Around the end of the nineteenth century the Royal Army Medical corps was formed. Working in conjunction with the Red Cross and the St John's Ambulance Brigade, the corps established regimental aid posts, field dressing stations and clearing hospitals as near to battlefields as possible. If further treatment was needed the wounded men were shipped back to hospitals in Britain. Often working in terrible conditions, these brave men and woman of the RAMC worked in posts that were often converted cottages or cowsheds. These buildings were made as sterile as possible, where staff worked hour after hour bandaging wounds and amputating limbs.

By July 1916 women, who were trained nurses, were being sent to the Front, and one of them was simply known as Nurse Ryalls of Newhill, Wath upon Dearne. She wrote to her brother and sister in Rotherham in July 1916 describing her experiences on the front line. She complained that after a heavy battle with large numbers of wounded men it was almost impossible to get them off the battlefield. Nurse Ryalls was attached to a first aid post that was based in 'a school yard somewhere in France'. She described how, soon after her arrival, she took off the dressing of a young Rotherham soldier, who had part of his elbow blown away. She wrote that 'it looked awful, but I got

Wounded Great War soldiers, some blinded by the use of gas

over it because I didn't have time to think about it'. She relates to her siblings:

> *There were others patiently waiting to be attended to and I think in such circumstances as these, one can see the true pluck and courage of the British Tommy, Everyone worked hard and when all were attended to, and we looked in silence around [...] We had dealt with 134 wounded, among whom were several Germans. Under a shed in the school yard lay five men who died after being brought in. They were later reverently buried in the cemetery.*

She admitted that on many occasions wounded men were often left lying on the floor, still dressed in their soaked and muddy clothes, waiting to be attended to. Some were delirious, whilst other lay 'in silent patience'. In her letter Nurse Ryalls paid particular tribute to the stretcher-bearers, having to go out in the dark and try to locate the wounded men and bring them back for treatment. Inevitably on the field of battle, the wounded men lying in No-Man's-Land could only be removed at night by stretcher-bearers risking shells and being shot at by snipers. Advancing troops were not allowed to care for their fallen comrades, although most carried a basic first aid kit.

The dangers that stretcher-bearers faced on a daily basis was reported with the death of one such man from Rotherham, Private Arthur Sanderson. Prior to enlistment he had lived on Bradgate Road with his father and mother, John and Christiana Sanderson. He also had two brothers, George aged 22 and Wilfred aged 26, and two sisters, Eliza and Lillian aged 14 and 12. Private Sanderson enlisted at Rotherham on 10 December 1915. During the war he married and he and his wife, Emily, went to live in a house on Peter Street, Kimberworth. He later joined the RAMC on 7 August 1916 and

Soldiers searching for bodies after a battle

undertook what was described as 'sterling work' until twenty months later when he was killed by gunshot wounds to the face and head. His family were notified that he had died on 2 May 1918, while helping to take a wounded soldier off the battlefield. His effects were later sent to his wife on 24 August 1918. They consisted of a broken watch, a wallet, a notebook, scissors, a knife, a ring and three coins. On Armistice Day the widow was informed that she had been awarded a pension for herself of 13s 9d a week.

Another man who was recognised for his bravery on the field was Private Alfred Scholes who was awarded the DCM in September 1916 for:

> *Conspicuous gallantry as a stretcher bearer during operations.*
> *He searched for and tended the wounded in the open, under heavy*
> *shell fire where he exhibited an utter contempt for danger.*

Prior to enlisting he had lived with his sister on Rawmarsh Road, Rotherham. But the highest honour was reserved for Sergeant Frank Jessop of France Street, Parkgate. His father, Pioneer Jessop was in the Territorials for thirty-six years and Sergeant Jessop himself had also served for twenty-three years in the same regiment. He left England in

Men would lie injured in No-Man's-Land, in conditions like these, waiting for rescue

April 1915 for the continent and was first mentioned in dispatches for 'good work' on 10 and 11 July of that year, during what was described as 'the heaviest bombardment of the British lines'. Sergeant Jessop was awarded the DCM on 19 December 1915 and the citation was for conspicuous gallantry when:

Although severely shaken by the explosion of a shell close to the dressing station, he refused to go to hospital, and for some time afterwards performed his duties as usual, showing an unremitting care and attention to other wounded men.

The DCM clasp was also awarded to him and this was followed by the Croix de Guerre, which was only granted for deeds of extraordinary bravery. The announcement of the award was made in the *Rotherham Advertiser* in May 1917

After large battles there were many wounded soldiers forced to lie where they fell, often in the greatest agony, until medical help could reach them. Some wounded men dragged themselves into shell holes to try to escape snipers, but there was a danger that they could be sucked into the mud and drowned. There were many instances of the courageous doctors of the RAMC risking their necks by going out to tend to wounded men where they lay. There they would minister to those who could not wait to be brought into the first aid post. Injured men in No-Man's-Land had to survive snipers and bombs in the best way that they could. One letter to the *Advertiser* in May 1916 described how an unnamed Rotherham man had been left on the battlefield all day before being rescued and brought into the aid post. He was forced to lie still in No-Man's-Land from 8am, when had been shot, until dark. He said:

There were half-a-dozen others there too, all wounded that lay there all day. Those snipers shoved lead into anything that showed signs of life. The chap next to me was badly hit and inclined to move. I warned him twice to lie flat and not squirm as the Germans were watching for any movement, and would plug him wounded or not. He stuck it steady for four hours, and then he tried to roll over and showed a shoulder and he got it. As soon as the snipers could not see me after dark, I started to drag myself

back to our trenches and met some of the boys sent out to look for
us.

Working in the terrible conditions of the battlefield the stretcher-bearers had to remove the men as best they could. In good conditions two men could carry an injured man, but in the mud it would often take four. The bravery of these men was never in doubt and their heroism was noted from the early years of the war. The war diary records that on 13 July 1915, an appendix report from Lieutenant General Charles Rose noted that 'I also wish to bring to notice the heroic manner in which the whole of the stretcher-bearers of the battalion performed their duties in dressing and carrying out the wounded men.'

As numbers of wounded men increased it was noted that many of them had only been in battle for just a few weeks. The reality was that many Rotherham men who went in their thousands to enlist had never fired a gun or seen comrades blown to bits. Witnessing such acts at the front line, combined with the horrendous shelling that went on for hours at a time, resulted in a mental illness called 'shell shock'. This psychosomatic disorder left men unable to sleep, walk or talk and the inevitable loss of self control. It was eventually recognised that, if not treated, the condition could become chronic. Nevertheless, in the early years of the war, in great ignorance such men were thought of as cowards and shot. Little was written about or spoken of shell shock as it was not properly understood in the Great War, and the men who were suffering from it were simply labelled 'lunatics'.

But ironically, in Rotherham, this disorder among wounded men was first noted by the workhouse officials. The guardian minutes report, as early as September 1916, that some returning soldiers who had come back to the town had exhibited some 'mental agitation'. It was recorded that 'more than a small number of men have become lunatics, whilst serving their country'. Historically, all people diagnosed as having any kind of mental illness were usually treated in the hospital wards of local workhouses. Therefore, Rotherham medical officers had to treat growing numbers of men suffering from shell shock. No longer able to carry out their duties, they were returned to the town and sent to the workhouse lunatic wards. The medical officers recognised that shell shock could not be put into the same category of the people that they called lunatics. As a result, the Rotherham Guardians requested the

Poor Law Board to arrange for the men to be sent into specialist mental hospitals rather than workhouse asylums. They put forward the argument that these men had suffered as a result of fighting for their country, and that as such they did not come under the auspices of the Poor Law. However, there was little response and three months later they were again requesting the Poor Law Board to lobby the government to ensure that such men should be supported by the state and not at the cost of local ratepayers.

At a time when military authorities took the stand that these soldiers were cowards who were trying to get out of fighting, it is a comfort to know that Rotherham recognised the need for these men to take a complete rest away from the front line. By 22 September 1917, it was announced in the local newspaper that a flag day for 'war broken men' would be held on Saturday 15 October. The *Advertiser* noted that it was hoped a collection would provide three beds at Lord Kitchener's Memorial Holiday House at Lowestoft for a period of twenty years. An amount of £954 was needed to secure these beds in order to send some of the Rotherham wounded soldiers suffering from this affliction. It was hoped the men would 'enjoy a holiday amid invigorating surroundings', which would rid them of this illness. The newspaper made a direct appeal to Rotherham 'on behalf of their own men whose health had been impaired in defending lives and homes'. Thankfully, modern medicine and psychiatry has all but eliminated this disabling illness, but in the years of the Great War, wounded soldiers with more physical injuries still had to be attended to.

It was recognised right from the outbreak of war that Rotherham would have to make arrangements for the reception of wounded soldiers, and once again it was the workhouse officials that noted the fact. In a meeting of the Rotherham Guardians at the workhouse on 14 September 1914, Lady Mabel Smith proposed that the Corporation be offered 100 beds at the workhouse. Lady Mabel was the daughter of Viscount Milton, who lived at Barnes Hall near Grenoside, and she was a large influence as a Rotherham Guardian, who later became an avid socialist. She worked tirelessly to prepare the hospital wing and by February 1917 the whole of E block was handed over to the military for injured Rotherham soldiers. The wing was renamed the Auxiliary Military Hospital. The workhouse guardian minutes state that by 13

April 1917, three VAD nurses were employed to work at the hospital, and during the years of the Great War the wing was in constant use. At the end of the war it was found that from its opening on 24 April 1917 to June 1918, a total of 670 admissions had passed through its doors. There was also a Red Cross ward allocated at the Rotherham Hospital, which also received large numbers of wounded and sick men.

As the streets of the town were filled with wounded soldiers, there were reports that some of the men were greeted by clapping from grateful citizens. Yet it was commented on 29 May 1915 that 'few people in the town were actually aware that there were twenty wounded soldiers in the Rotherham Hospital'. When it became known an appeal was inserted in the *Advertiser* requesting that anyone wishing to lend a helping hand to these brave men could put their cars at their disposal. Gifts of soap, cigarettes and sweets were also requested and provided by the people of Rotherham. Generally speaking the wounded soldiers who returned to the town were very well treated, but when the men

Doncastergate as it is today

were asked to attend recruitment campaigns, no provision had been made for their transportation in June 1915. A letter was sent to the editor of the *Advertiser* condemning the fact that local organisers had made no arrangements for the journey into and out of the town centre. The letter pointed out that some of these soldiers were:

> *[...] on crutches and with the aid of sticks were hobbling down Doncastergate in the midst of a throng of people. They would have had to hobble the whole way [...] had not some private individuals, touched by their incapacitated appearance 'clubbed up' and paid for a taxi cab.*

Returning the disabled men back to the hospital was just as humiliating. It appears that when they climbed on board a tram the car conductor came and demanded their fare. Only then was it noted that none of the soldiers had any money on them. Rather than see them turned off the cab, the fare was paid by a private individual. Calling it 'a disgrace to the town', the unnamed correspondent requested that better arrangements be made for these men in future. By the following year, better treatment was rightly given. It was reported on 28 September 1916 that wounded soldiers from the Oakwood VAD hospital were entertained by a bowling competition on the Boston Park green. Tea was provided and the president of the club, Mr Hampshire, stated that he was delighted to welcome the men on the fourth occasion of that season. Cigarettes were distributed and the men were invited to take turns in a competition.

One such wounded soldier who returned to Rotherham was Corporal J. Nixon, who had been sent home to recuperate after a shell exploded near him. He arrived in February 1915, with a large wound in his leg, to find his friend Private E. Dyson already home on leave at the same time. Interviewed by a reporter, Corporal Nixon told him that he had been with the 15th Lancers and was stationed in India at the outbreak of the war. When war was declared he was sent to France as a dispatch rider with the Sherwood Foresters, where the biggest danger he had to face was from snipers. This was a particularly harrowing role and he told the reporter that he had:

> *[...] been through a large share of the fighting and had several narrow escapes from injury. One of the chief dangers we have to*

encounter was that of snipers and these men were usually cunningly concealed. They follow our men about with their guns and can effect a considerable loss before they are discovered. They get well behind the English lines and are impossible to trace.

Corporal Nixon related how one such sniper followed him for many miles, but he could not muster sufficient courage to attack him. He stated that he had seen some horrific sights as being 'terrible in the extreme' whilst he had been fighting and was glad to be home on leave. His friend Private Dyson belonged to the 2nd Kings Own Yorkshire Light Infantry and he too had been through many battles and escaped harm. He also told the reporter that he was lucky and that he too had some very narrow escapes. Private Dyson described how he had lost comrades either side of him. The weather was the biggest difficulty he had experienced, and was at that time suffering from frostbitten feet brought on by standing in cold and wet trenches. Both men were expected to return back to the fighting line as soon as they had recovered from their injuries.

Throughout the years of the Great War the streets of Rotherham were filled with wounded men who were dealt with very leniently by police constables. From the early months of the war Mr Weatherhogg informed his officers that the men were not to be interfered with 'unless it was absolutely necessary'. He specifically mentioned that 'no soldiers are be arrested, unless they were found committing an extremely serious offence'. In order to deal with any infringements, a squad of military police had been attached to the police station that assisted in all matters dealing with the soldiers of the town.

CHAPTER 8

The Rotherham police force

During the war years the police station and courthouse were situated at the now empty premises on Frederick Street. At the time of the outbreak of war, the strength of the force included a chief constable, Mr E. Weatherhogg and chief inspector, Mr J. Altoft. Other ranks included four inspectors named Spencer, Green, Tipping and White, nine sergeants and sixty-nine constables. Once war was declared the Rotherham police had all leaves of absence cancelled and all those members of the force who were already on leave had to return to duty. In June 1915 the right of any police officer to retire was suspended for the duration of the war. The Police and Watch Committee empowered

The present site of Frederick Police Station and courts

Mr Weatherhogg to engage a sufficient number of special constables to deal with any emergency that arose. These early specials were to be limited to 100 men, who were paid 6d an hour and given a boot allowance. They would also be used to replace any members of the force who wished to enlist. Notice had already been received by the chief constable 'that he give every possible facility to the men of the force who were reservists, to join the colours with the least possible delay'.

One of the first police officers to enlist was Constable Edwin James, who had lodged with Mr and Mrs Harrison at William Street, Wellgate. He had for many years been a member of the Territorial Army at Rotherham and had trained with them as a Saturday Soldier as they were commonly called. Only two weeks prior to the war being announced, PC James had transferred to Sheffield City Police. There he enlisted with the 2nd battalion of the Coldstream Guards. In his capacity as a reserve with the territorials, PC James was reported to be a crack shot, having won the 1911 Aldershot Command Shooting Championship. Because of his experience as a Territorial, Private James was sent to France with the British Expeditionary Force. He took part in much of the fighting and escaped injury until 14 September 1914, when he was shot. He told Mrs Harrison, his former landlady:

Never did I dream when leaving England that I should experience such a terrible time and I shall never forget the day I was wounded. Syd Crieb a Sheffield constable carried me off the battlefield to a place of safety, as shells were bursting galore.

But when Private James arrived at a field hospital he found there was no nursing staff there. He described the nightmare situation:

The medical officers and stretcher-bearers had been captured, and the wounded had to look out for themselves. I was hungry and exhausted as no supplies had reached us for three days. There was no safety for the wounded, for the Germans shelled all the hospitals, it was terrible.

Finally a motor ambulance arrived and took the wounded men to a French railway station before being taken to a hospital in Birmingham. Private James described how it was very painful for the wounded to be shaken about in the back of these lorries, but nevertheless considered themselves lucky to have escaped the shelling for a while. He also told his former landlady that many of the wounds the men received were from shrapnel, and that this was one of the most effective weapons in the German armoury. One piece of this heavy metal could shred a person, leaving terrible wounds

On the very day that war was declared a confidential memo from the Secretary of State was issued to Mr Weatherhogg, urging that all members of the Rotherham force co-operate with the military authorities 'in any manner in which they require assistance'.[24] The secretary also requested that the police help speed along the process of the mobilisation of troops. Movement of these soldiers was adding pressure at the Rotherham railway stations. On 27 August 1914, the chief constable ordered a number of men to be sent to the Masbrough Midland station. There were large numbers of recruits leaving that day between 5pm and 6pm, and it was expected that an equally large numbers of relatives would attend the station to see the men off. Several constables were sent to keep order. Pressure increased as the mobilisation of troops out of Rotherham progressed. On 29 August 1914, more police officers were required at Masbrough station, once again as large number of trains were expected. The military had previously agreed with the Rotherham police force that Masbrough

A piece of shrapnel – this heavy metal can cause terrible injuries when it impacts with a body.

The land at the side of Masbrough Station (now built on) where it is possible the horses were exercised on their way to war

Masbrough Station where relatives would say goodbye to loved ones on their way to war

station could be used to exercise horses of the cavalry units. They were allowed to take their horses out of the wagons and water them at Masbrough before pressing on to their destination. During the early years of the war many trains would be delayed for ordinary people as the needs of the military took precedence.

In January 1915 the chief constable had the sad duty of informing his men of the death of a former police constable at the morning drill held in the parade room. Private Nicholson was one of the first police deaths to have been reported on 27 December 1914. Many men were not familiar with his name as he had left the to join the force in Liverpool in 1913, and had enlisted there. The chief constable told his men that, nevertheless, he was a former colleague and his wife's mother still lived at Foundry Street, Masbrough. There is little doubt that Mr Weatherhogg would have sent a letter of condolence to the mother of a former colleague. Later that year he had the sad duty once again to inform his men of the death of Sergeant William McLellan, who died of his wounds on 20 July 1915. On the outbreak of war the former police constable immediately enlisted with the Lancaster Fusiliers on 6 August 1914. He had joined the Rotherham police force only in July of that year and had been one of the first of nine members of the force who had enlisted. Mr Weatherhogg told his men that all the others were still fighting in France. Private McLellan had proved to be a popular soldier with both his comrades and his superior officers, and quickly rose to the rank of sergeant. When he was killed, Sergeant McLellan was only 29 and left a widow and three children in Rotherham. Ironically, just before he died he had sent a letter to his wife to tell her he 'was safe and in the best of health'. He said that:

Devastated French houses in the Great War

405. La Guerre 1914-15 - CARENCY (P.-de-C.) - Maisons bombardées. R. P. Paris
Visé Paris 405

I have had the Rotherham paper once or twice and I was sorry to read about the disgraceful rioting. It would be better if those roughs were to come out here and riot against the Germans. I have met a good many Rotherham men, they are a fine lot of uncomplaining fellows. I have not heard any news of the men who left the force when war broke out. I hope they are going on well.

Sergeant McLellan had told his wife about the devastation left by the shelling of houses in the towns and villages through which the battalion had passed. He said that in the houses 'the meals were still on the table, as the owners had to make a hasty exit to escape with their lives'. He closed with a post script that stated: 'I hope soon to be home again and to take up police duty, as it is less exciting than this.' In November 1915, several more police constables went to enlist and Mr Weatherhogg called out their names in the parade room. He informed his men that former constables Pratt, Cade, Downing, Small and Briddon had enlisted in various units and that some had joined the Military Mounted Police for the duration. As was usual by now their place was taken by the special constables.

From the early days of the war, regular memorandums were sent to the police station on Frederick Street asking the men to be vigilant in detecting anything or anyone that would come under the category of spying for the enemy. Only after the war the *Advertiser* revealed that a group of actual spies had been arrested in the town. In March 1918 a group of music hall entertainers were later found to be German spies. No details were given apart from the fact that they had been arrested and dealt with.

The biggest impact made on the police at Rotherham during the years of the Great War was on 8 August 1914 when the Defence of the Realm Act (DORA) came into place. Mr Weatherhogg informed his officers that from that day the Act gave them powers to arrest without a warrant men and women acting 'in a manner detrimental to public safety'.[26] Although there is little in the inspectors' memorandum book about anyone arrested for such activities, in February 1916 it was reported that treasonous leaflets were circulating in the industrial parts of Rawmarsh and Parkgate. These leaflets were allegedly from the Kaiser himself, in the form of a letter asking British workers to 'object to the war and to refuse to fight'. A copy of the letter was taken to the police station. The *Advertiser* questioned how these leaflets were delivered in the first place among Rotherham people whose 'loyalty is unquestioned'.

On 29 August 1915, Major General Sir J. H. Trotter, the Secretary of State, informed the Rotherham police force that 'no sketches or photographs were to be made of military camps, buildings occupied by the military or any troop activities'.[27] The following month another letter arrived warning the town council that the Admiralty had been advised that 'German agents from neutral countries had been infiltrating large armament manufacturers'. They were believed to be planning to damage or destroy such industries and asked the Rotherham police to be especially vigilant. All local manufacturers were warned to 'take all possible guard against such agents', and were to 'give all possible assistance to the military authorities by identifying such individuals'.

Perhaps the biggest problem that the police of Rotherham had to face was not that of spies but when instructions were issued by DORA about restrictions on the sale of alcohol. This was a matter that annoyed not only the public but the owners of hotels and public houses of the town, as it obviously affected their livelihood. In May 1915 a total prohibition of alcohol was called for by the Masbrough Wesleyan Church. Reverend J. Mathewman, whilst speaking of England stated that:

> *The fact was that she was weak and wobbling when dealing with the enemy within the gates. Drink had hindered recruiting and had spoiled recruits when they had enlisted. It was ruining the homes of men who had gone to serve. Today the convalescent soldiers were prolonging their convalescence owing to the drink. I plead for voluntary abstinence on the part of the strong and compulsory prohibition on the part of the weak.*

It was estimated that in the early months of 1915 there were seventy fully licensed public houses as well as fifty-seven beer houses in and around the borough of Rotherham. It was widely known that the king himself, in the first few months of the war, had sworn off alcohol for the duration. The leading advocates of the Temperance Movement agreed that soldiers and sailors should emulate his example. In March

1915, the sale of intoxicating liquors on licensed premises all over the country were limited under DORA. The Rotherham chief inspector was informed that pubs and beer house could only open between 12 noon to 1pm and 6pm to 9pm, and he urged his men to be vigilant in ensuring that the Act was carefully adhered to. The *Advertiser* noted that even as late as 22 November 1915 the people of the town 'could hardly accept this loss of drinking time'. Seven months after the restricted hours had been introduced it was noted that:

> *Not a few people of the town were at a loss to account for the closed doors in the bars and hotels of the town, and every hotel and innkeeper had a disconsolate appearance at his closed premises.*

One particular class of persons to which the restriction was aimed was the soldiers themselves. The Act clearly specified that alcohol could only be supplied during the designated hours. It stated that 'any license holder, including off license sales, were not to supply soldiers with intoxicating liquor except during such times'. Another danger of alcohol was aimed at the workers themselves, as it was felt that drinking men slowed up the production of shells and ammunition. A Rotherham Labour MP, Captain Kelley, wrote a letter to his constituents in the town during the following month. Speaking directly to 'his friends in the trade', he stated that he was sure they were as loyal as any of His Majesty's subjects and anxious to answer Sir John French's calls for more armaments. He said: 'We are told that workmen are delaying the manufacture of armaments to the serious detriment of our lads in the trenches, by the sale of intoxicating drinks.' He concluded his letter by using the patriotic propaganda in wide circulation of the time, stating that:

> *I therefore appeal to everyone in the trade who constitutes himself or herself as a national guard, nay an Imperial guard against the weakness of those workmen who have not the strength of will of their own, to know that the country and our brave men are crying out in pathetic appeals for the result of their labour to help those who are giving freely of their lives to defeat our enemy, who have no respect for our women and children of our splendid Allies and*

A typical Great War tin in which gifts were sent to soldiers at the Front.

> *who, if not beaten will outrage our wives, mothers and daughter*
> *of our own people as they have done to our Allies.*

The ban on sales affected the very first Easter holiday after the war began, which was described by a reporter as being 'very quiet indeed'. He stated that the early closing hours had emptied the streets of the town and as a consequence gas was now being reduced in the centre of town after 9pm. The *Advertiser* confidently stated that 'the people of the town had accepted the reduced sale of alcohol with good grace'. Also, as a result of this curfew, the shopkeepers of the town had reported that money was more plentiful than previously and they had record sales. The shops had long supported the boys on the front line, and regular gifts of sweets, tobacco and chocolate were sent from the town. The same reporter stated that the news was 'at least worth recording in order that it might reach the eyes of the Germans, who seemed to think that the damage caused by their submarines are surely causing a famine in Old England'.

Nevertheless, whatever their private thoughts, the Rotherham police had to be vigilant to enforce the reduced licensing laws. A case was brought before the Rotherham Police Court on 28 August 1915 concerning an off license on Wortley Road where a woman had been seen selling beer to a soldier at 2pm on Sunday 1 August, contrary to DORA. The serviceman had been seen coming out of her premises with a jug of beer on the day in question. The police officer took him back into the premises and spoke to the woman in charge. She stated that she was so busy she hadn't noticed the time and told the constable that she was a widow who was looking after her former husband's business. Her husband had died on 29 July and the licence had only been transferred to her two or three days before. The offence had occurred the day after the Act had been amended, and so she was ordered just to pay the court costs.

As well as the reduced hours, even the natural kindness of buying a serviceman a drink whilst on leave in the town was condemned. In one letter to the editor of the local newspaper, a girl signing herself 'a sailor's daughter' was published on 9 November 1915, condemns the practise, asking when a serviceman has been away so long from drink, and the public try to press it on him, 'how is he to resist?' She urged that instead of buying the soldier alcohol that well-wishers buy him some warm wearing apparel that he can enjoy when he is back in the trenches. It is not recorded what the soldiers themselves thought about this idea, but a furore occurred later the same month when the Rotherham Temperance Movement condemned the rum ration that was issued not only to sailors at sea but also the soldiers in the trenches. Three soldiers wrote to the editor of the *Advertiser* from the front line on 11 December 1915 to condemn the decision. Signallers C. Griffiths, A. Bailey and M. Roebuck wrote that the person who had condemned the serving of the rum should:

Imagine himself in the trenches knee deep in mud, clapping his hands and stamping his feet to keep warm. Can he imagine himself coming off patrol, where he has had to creep in sludge and water for a matter of two hours, or perhaps had to lie in one place until the clothes he has on are frozen. If these feelings could be transferred to him, I am sure he would be making his way to the nearest liquor house as fast as he could.

Another soldier, Private W. May, also criticised the people who objected to the rum ration. In a letter to his wife written on 12 February 1915, he told her that 'if some of the people who stand at home and talk, would come out here and do some fighting instead of talking about us getting a drop of rum, the war would soon be over and let the poor beggars get home again'.

Naturally criminals did not take a holiday during wartime and the Rotherham police were kept busy throughout the Great War, but the greatest crime they had to deal with was from young people. On 29 March 1909, Rotherham Juvenile Court had been established to deal specifically with offenders under 16 years of age. One of the largest complaints made during the war years was the number of young men attending court for gambling in the street. Many of these offenders were young boys from 13 to 17 and it was estimated that for every case brought to court, at least half-a-dozen other people escaped. Even young girls had been found in these groups, and the lack of parental control was blamed for this 'growing evil'. One unnamed boy, aged 13, who appeared in the juvenile court on 8 August 1914, told magistrates that he was not working and the only money he had gathered was the odd copper or two from relatives. His mother also attended the court and she told the magistrates that he had not been given any money by her. The magistrate responded that as a parent 'she should know where her son got his money from if she was doing her duty correctly'. Throughout the war years gambling increased and Superintendent Haynes was forced to raid gambling schools of pitch and toss in September 1915 when over thirty men and boys were brought before the magistrates. The chief constable pointed out that for many of the men brought in for gambling, they usually had a wife and children reliant on the money that they were throwing away. He asked the magistrates to clamp down on this growing nuisance by imposing much heavier fines.

When the war began all the police had their leave cancelled and so it was with some gratitude that on Saturday 1 September 1918, with the end of hostilities in sight, that the whole of the Rotherham police force was given a day off to celebrate. For one day only the force was manned by special constables who took over all the patrols. It was seen as a great success, which was evident when not one person was brought before the magistrates court on the following Monday morning.

CHAPTER 9

The end of the war

We know now that 1918 was the last year of the war, but the men in the trenches must have wondered how much longer the massacre would continue. The war diaries show that the total of men killed during 1917 was twenty-six officers and 1,180 other ranks.[30] In Rotherham, the end of the war was announced by an unnamed soldier on 12 October 1918, who told his parents:

> *By the time you receive this, I think you will have some very good news, so start airing and pressing my civvies – no joking or jesting. I feel as happy as a lark. Order my Christmas dinner, because I have great hopes of finishing before then.*

By the time the armistice had been signed, celebrations in Rotherham were in full swing. Crowds gathered in College Square to hear the Salvation Army band play, and flags and bunting covered most of the houses in the town. But the most significant change was when the church bells of the parish church began to ring out. It had been agreed early in the war that the bells would only be rung to notify people of an invasion or to celebrate at the end of hostilities. Fairy lights joined streets lights for the first time in four years, and bonfires were lit on which effigies of the kaiser were burned. But in the midst of the most joyful celebrations, as more and more Rotherham men returned back to the town, stories were still heard of the suffering of men who been prisoners-of-war. It quickly became very obvious that one of the worst was the camp at Doeberitz, where Harry Abel had been imprisoned.

Rotherham Parish Church undergoing repairs in 2011/12

The camp was situated northwest of Potsdam and had been set up by the Germans in 1915. No account was made for the large numbers of men who were being imprisoned there and the overcrowding at the camp, resulting in prisoners sleeping in huts and tents with little to keep them warm. Prisoners returning to Rotherham said that while there the food was basic and disease in the camp was rife.

One ex-prisoner-of-war, Private Brian Sugden of Belmont Street, Rotherham, angrily spoke about his experiences in another camp at Gustrow in Germany, where the men had also been treated like animals. He told the *Advertiser* that when he had been taken prisoner on 31 October 1914, he weighed 12 stone 4 pounds, but on his return to Rotherham he weighed only 8 stone. Private Sugden had been an experienced soldier and had served in the army for sixteen years before war broke out. When war was declared he enlisted and went to France with his regiment, the North Lancasters. He fought in the battle of Mons but had been captured along with thousands of other men who had found themselves cut off. The prisoners were quickly rounded up by the Germans and placed on a forced march to Lille. Many were wounded, yet they were subjected to kicks from guards on the journey. On arrival at Lille they were exhibited in the marketplace, but the French people were sympathetic towards the prisoners and tried to give them food. They were then placed in cattle trucks for the journey to the camp at Gustrow. On the way, there were several stops where, again, they were used as exhibits. Private Sugden reported that the German people would spit at them and some threw stones at the 'English swine'. Before they reached the camp they went to Hamburg, where they were subjected to a tirade from a German general. Few prisoners could speak German but there was no doubting the content of his speech, which was accompanied by hog-like grunts. When they arrived at the camp they were put to work, clearing up the bombed German cities and towns.

Private Sugden told the reporter about one of his comrades in the camp another Rotherham soldier, Private Frank Woodward of the Coldstream Guards. The two men became firm friends as they struggled to deal with conditions. They were forced to lie on damp straw with few blankets, which they soon found to be alive with vermin. The cold weather was very intense and as a result many lost

Bombed-out churches in towns and cities during the Great War

fingers and toes through frostbite. The food was so bad that many prisoners resorted to eating potato peelings left by the guards. Matters started to slightly improve as packages from home were sent through the Red Cross. Private Sugden told a reporter that one disturbing feature of prison life in Gustrow camp was the disappearance of prisoners who would go to bed and never be seen again. Unfortunately, his comrade Frank Woodward died in the prison camp a few days before the armistice was signed. It was reported that when he arrived back in Rotherham he was one of the lucky ones who found his wife eagerly awaiting his return. She too had struggled, whilst her husband had been a prisoner, on the slender income allowed to wives of men who had been captured. Nevertheless, the *Advertiser* told its readers that 'she had kept the home together, keeping it scrupulously warm and cosy as she waited for her husband's return'.

Stories about the treatment of British and Allied prisoners in the Great War prompted a committee to hold an inquiry before the armistice was even signed. Interviews were held with repatriated prisoners by examiners appointed by the committee, about the treatment they had suffered when they had been captured. One of the cases was of a Rotherham man, Lance Corporal John Oliver Card, who was killed whilst kept prisoner at Poilecourt camp, on 25 August 1918. The camp was situated just behind the German lines, about 16km north of Rheims. Details of their son's death were given in January of the following year to his parents at Henley Grove, Rotherham, from Company Sergeant Major R. Huitt. He wrote to Mr and Mrs Charles Card telling them that on the morning of his death their son had risen and gone to the latrines, which were situated about 120 yards from his hut. On reaching the hut he was stopped by a German guard, who without provocation started hitting him with a stick. When Lance Corporal Card raised his arm to protect himself, the German sentry drew out his pistol and shot him. The guard made the excuse that the prisoner had attempted to hit him, but another prisoner had witnessed the unprovoked attack. Lance Corporal Card was taken to a small hospital in the camp, where he was attended by an RAMC corporal, but he passed away about two hours later. Before he died, he recounted the incident to Sergeant Major Huitt, who later challenged the German officer in charge of the camp. The sergeant major demanded justice for Lance Corporal Card, but he told the parents the camp commander 'would not listen to me'.

Funeral in a prison-of-war camp

He told the bereaved parents that their son's body had been buried at Poilecourt in the German Military cemetery there, and that seven of his pals were allowed to attend the funeral under an armed escort. Sergeant Major Huitt told Mr and Mrs Card that he had carried out the service in the best way he could, under the circumstances. He stated that his grave was marked with their son's name and regiment as he told them:

It is really a very sad affair when one recalls it, as Lance Corporal Card was considered one of the best men in the camp. We felt it was very hard for him to be put to death in such a brutal way, after sharing his hardships with us the few months we were all prisoners together. I feel certain that all the men join me in expressing our deepest sympathy to you. His private belongings were given to one of his pals belonging to the same regiment, so I trust you will receive them alright.

So incensed was Sergeant Major Huitt that as soon as he was released from the camp and arrived back in England, he put the case to the Prisoners-of-War Committee enquiry, which was being held at Dover. He was summoned to give evidence in the case of Lance Corporal Card and Major Huitt promised his parents that 'I will write to you if I hear any further about the case'. Sadly, Lance Corporal Card was only 22 years of age, and like many others had been employed at the Rotherham Main Colliery before he enlisted in August 1914. During the war he had been wounded twice, and it was on his third time in France when he was taken prisoner on 27 May 1918. His was not the only case,

Temporary wooden crosses on Great War graves

The Crofts, Rotherham as it is today

and similar stories were heard in Rotherham from other prisoners-of-war returning to the town.

Towards the end of the war many Rotherham families found out what had actually happened to their relatives who had been killed in action. At first it was the responsibility of the battalion to bury a body, and so when a dead soldier was found after a battle, if possible he would usually be identified by an NCO. Then the body would be quickly buried in a temporary grave just marked with their names on wooden crosses. The task of excavating and re-burying the bodies of men killed in battle in the military cemeteries was described in August 1918 by Private T. C. White, formerly of the Crofts, Rotherham. He had belonged to the 3rd Labour Corp, a forerunner of the Royal Pioneer Corps and his task was to exhume the bodies of soldiers buried on the battlefield, most of whom were buried where they fell. He re-assured the people of Rotherham that their relatives' bodies had always received the utmost respect, in order to 'lay their dear ones comfortably,

A military cemetery in Ypres as it looks today – the graves are regularly inspected and cared for and can be visited by relatives

where they will forever rest in peace'. Private White described how the bodies were carefully disinterred and then laid out on stretchers before being placed on transport wagons, where they were taken to official cemeteries. They were then placed in another grave with a wooden cross bearing the name, number and battalion of each man placed at the head. These would eventually be replaced by a more permanent memorial. Private White told the *Rotherham Advertiser* in a letter to the editor:

> It is one thing to dig graves at home for the reception of coffins, but it is another thing to exhume bodies here and rebury them. It is a gruesome job to do and I can assure you that none but men with iron nerves and hearts of stone can stand the strain. But the more we do, the more we get hardened into it, knowing that it is the last tribute we can pay to our noble heroes.

The work of finding war heroes continues to this day. Long after the war, known battlefields are still being searched by military archaeologists and any remains that can be identified are then re-interred in the military cemeteries and the bodies named. In the Great War all soldiers who were missing and had no known graves were not forgotten. Their names were engraved on the major war memorials. One beautiful monument is the Menin Gate, which holds the names of more than 54,000 officers and men whose bodies were never found. Above the gate is a tablet that reads:

> *To the Armies of the British Empire who stood here from 1914 – 1918 and to those of their dead who have no known grave.*

As 'the war to end all wars' came to an end there was a question as to which regiment had held the most men of Rotherham. The *Advertiser*, as usual, was able to answer the question. The paper noted that most of the local soldiers wore the badge of the York and Lancaster Regiment. Two battalions, the 1/5th and 2/5th Territorials, were raised in the town and the outlying districts. These were followed by further battalions, which probably contained more local men than any other unit in the army, The men of Rotherham contributed to the Connaught Rangers, the 7th Munsters, the Durham Light Infantry, the West Yorkshire, the Green Howards and the West Riding Regiment, as well as the King's Own Yorkshire Light Infantry. Well over a thousand men joined the naval battalions and two regiments that were specially raised in the town were the Rotherham Howitzer Brigade and the Heavy Battery. The newspaper makes no mention of the Royal Flying Corps at that time, which was re-named the Royal Air Force in April 1918, and was instrumental in the next war. Nevertheless, it was estimated that at least 29,000 Rotherham men had enlisted from the town, although the full total might never be known due to local men joining other units belonging to the empire. There were Rotherham men in the Canadian, South African and Australian battalions. What was never in any doubt was the absolute and complete bravery of the men of Rotherham.

An article printed in the *Rotherham Advertiser* of 16 November 1918 truly counted the cost to the town of men killed in action. The newspaper states that 'the loyalty of the borough and district was manifest right from the start'. Practically as soon as war was declared:

The Menin Gate, Ypres – each night the traffic is stopped and the Last Post is sounded to remember the dead of the Great War

The people of the district had risen to the occasion and were ready for any demand which might be made upon them. No one could forget the recruiting scenes of those early days [...] During the 4th and 5th August 1914, many local reservists were called to the Colours and enthusiastic send offs marked their departure [...]Throughout August and September the men flocked in contingents from Silverwood and Dinnington, either brought in by motor bus or headed by a marching band. These were the men who two years later, were to earn undying fame on the Somme.

Thankfully many men did survive the war and one such was an experienced soldier named James William Porter. He had been just 18 years and 2 months when he enlisted in the King's Own Yorkshire Light Infantry on 13 April 1902. At the time he joined the army he was a single man, 5' 3" tall and weighing 112lb. He completed his medical at Sheffield on the day of his enlistment and was registered fit for duty. When he was released from the army service three years later, he was retained as a reservist. The 1911 census lists him as living at Psalter Lane, Rotherham, aged 27 years of age, with his wife, Sylvia Maude, aged 25. He was a labourer at Howells Steel Tube works at Wincobank, and at the time had two children, a son named after himself aged 3, and a daughter Alice Victoria aged 2. On the outbreak of war he was called to action and enlisted as a private once again in his old regiment in August 1914. Two months later, in October 1914, Private Porter received a bullet wound in the chest, which was not too serious and he was sent to a hospital in Le Havre, where he quickly recovered. Later he returned to the trenches and the local newspaper recorded that he had been 'in the thick of the fighting ever since'. In a letter to his mother, who by then had moved to Back Lane, Holmes, in March 1915, he told her that he had been

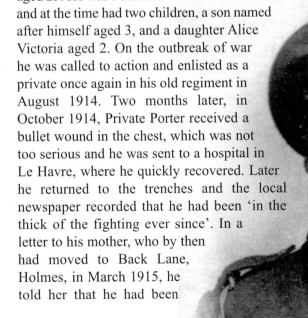

James William Porter

CENSUS OF ENGLAND AND WALES, 1911.

Before writing on this Schedule please, read the Examples and the Instructions given on the other side of the paper, as well as the headings of the Columns. The entries should be written in Ink.

The contents of the Schedule will be treated as confidential. Strict care will be taken that no information is disclosed with regard to individual persons. The returns are not to be used for proof of age, as in connection with Old Age Pensions, or for any other purpose than the preparation of Statistical Tables.

Number of Schedule. 299
(To be filled up by the Enumerator after collection)

NAME AND SURNAME	RELATIONSHIP to Head of Family.	AGE (last Birthday) and SEX.		PARTICULARS as to MARRIAGE.					PROFESSION or OCCUPATION of Persons aged ten years and upwards.			BIRTHPLACE of every person.	NATIONALITY of every Person born in a Foreign Country.	INFIRMITY.
		Ages Males.	Ages Females.		Completed years the present Marriage has lasted.	Total Children Born Alive.	Children still Living.	Children who have Died.	Personal Occupation.	Industry or Service with which worker is connected.	Whether Employer, Worker, or Own Account.	Whether Working at Home.			
1 Jarmore William Porter	Head	27		Married					Labourer at	Steel Works	Worker		forth Jorkshire		
2 Sylvia Maud Porter	Wife		25	Married	5	2	2	Thron					Weston Herefordshire		
3 James William Porter	Son	3 years 4 months		Single				1					Rotherham Yorkshire		
4 Alice Victoria Porter	Daughter		2 years	Single									Rotherham Yorkshire		
5															
6															
7															
8															
9															
10															
11															
12															
13															
14															
15															

(To be filled up by the Enumerator.)

Total.

	Males.	Females.	Persons.
	2	2	4

(To be filled up by the Head of Family or other person in occupation, or in charge, of this dwelling.)

Write below the Number of Rooms in this Dwelling (House, Tenement, or Apartment). Count the kitchen as a room but do not count scullery, landing, lobby, closet, bathroom; nor warehouse, office, shop.

4 Rooms

I declare that this Schedule is correctly filled up to the best of my knowledge and belief.

Signature James William Porter

Postal Address 130 Psalters Lane, Rotherham

1911 Census returns showing the family of James William Porter living on Psalters Lane, Rotherham

fighting for five months out of the seven in France and that he was:

[...] in good health and am getting fat in spite of having no teeth. This is a beautiful country and I would have liked to have seen it before the Germans ruined it. I would not like to think that our homes were like these.

Private Porter wrote another letter to his wife, which was printed in the *Advertiser*, two months later on 22 May 1915. He told her that two days ago he'd had a bath as he had 'fallen in a vat of beer'. He recounted how his chums had a good laugh at that, but added that it wasn't like good English beer or he might have 'stopped in a bit'. He added:

I hope that I am spared to come through this business alright, but somehow I doubt it. I am the only man in my platoon left who came out with the regiment from Dublin.

Thankfully, Private Porter did survive the war, as did his two brothers, who also both served. William Henry Porter,

James William Porter in Great War uniform

known as Harry joined up in the early days of 1914 and joined the York and Lancaster regiment. He was sent to Devon where, on 11 May 1915, he married a woman named Anna Howard. After the war, on 10 August 1929, Harry emigrated to Australia to start a new life. Their other brother, Walter, was a bit of a rogue and in 1909 was convicted of being involved in the sale of an overcoat. It was said that his family 'rarely spoke of the disgrace'. Nevertheless, he enlisted and went to war, where he did his patriotic duty and fought bravely. He too survived the war, but in his family's eyes he resumed his disgrace as it was rumoured that he left his wife and went on to commit bigamy. Thankfully, these brothers all survived the war and came back to Rotherham to resume their lives.

The journey back to the town of their birth was described by an unnamed soldier, who had served with the Territorial's in France and came home on 25 January 1919. In a journal entitled *Demobilisation: From Soldier to Civilian in Seven Days*, he describes the journey, including walking across No-Man's-Land in the Arras section at 2am in the morning. The sight of silhouetted crosses on isolated graves in the dark moonlight made a great impact on him and the other men. He reflected that 'to the mothers, wives and sweethearts of these men who had found their last resting place

William Henry Porter

in a foreign land, there would be no returning loved ones'. The soldier describes his feelings of great joy in returning back to the town of his birth, where he was welcomed by his family.

These are just some of the stories of Rotherham and its people in the Great War. Many did not return and those who did were changed forever. Some found it very difficult to resume their former lives after the horrors they had endured. Most, like Harry Abel, never spoke about their experiences. Others more able to articulate the terrible scenes they had witnessed summed it up:

My friend, you would not tell with such high zest
To children ardent for some desperate glory,
The old lie, Dulcie et Decorum est
Pro patria mori'

Wilfred Owen 1893-1918

Bibliography

Newspapers

Rotherham Advertiser

South Yorkshire Times

Rotherham Express

Books

Col H. C. Wyllie CB, *The York and Lancaster Regiment Vol II* (Ref 942.71/355.31)

Rotherham Annual 1915 – 1917

Rotherham Archives and Local Studies Service (RALS)

Board of Guardians Minutes, Ref 274-41 /25/26/27/28

Council Minute Book, Ref 61-C/1/2/10

Inspectors Memorandum Book, Ref 15-C /2/4

Inspectors Note Book, Ref 15-C/2/1

Watch and Fire Brigade Minutes, Ref 61-C/1/49/4

The York and Lancaster War Diary © Crown Copyright, The National Archives, Kew 16 INFANTRY BRIGADE: 2 Battalion York and Lancaster Regiment 1914 Aug. – 1919 Feb

Index

Able, Harry, 74–5, 132
Aisne, Battle of, 21, 31
Aizlewood, Major Leslie Peech, 92–3
Amphion, HMS, 18
Arnell, Clement, 19
Arras, Battle of, 27
    section, 132
Atlas Street, Canklow, 21
Aveluy Wood, 33

Back Lane, Holmes, 129
Bailey, Signaller A., 116–17
Bear Tree Road, Parkgate, 48
Belgium, 21, 31, 40
Belmont Street, 121
Berridge, Private Albert R., 50
Beverley, Private John Henry, 59–68, 70
Beverley, Private Joseph Arthur, 62–5, 70
Bird, Lieutenant Charles B., 92
Black Watch Regiment, 77
Bottom, Corporal John, 83–5
Bradgate Road, 99
Brailsford, Private Tom, 51
Bray, Private Arnold, 48
Brooke, Private Enoch, 21

Cambrai, battle of, 94
Cameron Highlanders, 31
Campsall, Private G., 31
Card, Lance Corporal John Oliver, 123–4
Carley, Harry, 79
Carpenter, Sergeant Frank, 32
Charles Street, Thornhill, 21
Chief Constable of Rotherham, 17, 22–4, 90, 107–11, 117
Claypit Lane, Sandhill, 36
Clifton Park, 23, 35, 70, 86
Cojeul British Cemetery, 27
College Square, 119
Coldstream Guards, 19, 108, 121
Colver, Captain, 22
Connaught Rangers, 127
Connelly, Private William Henry, 30
Coward, Alderman P. Bancroft, 16, 77
Crofts, 125

Dalton, Corporal Enoch, 53
Doeberitz Prison of War Camp, 75, 119
Dragoon Guards, 29
Drakeford, Mr Earnest, 76–7

Drill hall, 22–3
Duke of Cornwall's Life Infantry, 42
Duke of Wellingtons, 21
Durham Light Infantry, 127
Dyson, Private E., 105–6

Eastwood View, 30
East Yorkshire Regiment, 62, 68
Ernscliffe, Private F.G., 36

Finnie, Sergeant W., 31
Firth, Sapper, William Henry, 58
Firth, George Henry, 58
Forage Department Army Service Corps., 83
Foundry Street, Masbrough, 111
France Street, Parkgate, 100
Frederick Street, 78, 107, 112

Gent City Cemetery, Belgium, 40
Greasbrough Road, 74
Green Howard Regiment, 127
Green, Inspector of Rotherham Police, 72
Greenwood, Private Bert, 34
Greenwood, Private Isaac, 30–1
Griffiths, Signaller C., 116–17
Gustrow, Prison of War Camp, 121

Harpham, Private P., 47
Haywood, Private William, 46
Henry Street, 22
Hersin, France, 58
Holmes Lane, 34
Huitt, Company Sergeant Major R., 123–4

James, Constable Edward, 108–9
James, Lance Corporal Sydney, 25, 27

James Street, Masbrough, 83
Jessop, Sergeant Frank, 100–1
Jubb, Ernest, 16

Kelley, Captain, 114–15
Kenneth Street, 35
Keyworth, Signaller Horace, 35
Kimberworth Road, 35
King's Own Yorkshire Light Infantry, 17, 21, 27, 32, 106, 127, 129
King's Royal Rifles, 35
Kitchener, Lord, 17, 103

Labour Corp, 125
Lancaster Fusiliers, 111–12
Lawton, Private E., 46, 91
Lifeguards, 29
Limbach, Mr J.W., 79
Lindum Terrace, 90

Maiden, Samuel, 36, 39–40, 70
Masbrough Station, 109–10
May, Private W., 21, 117
McLellan, Sergeant William, 111
Midland Road, Masbrough, 51, 74
Military Mounted Police, 112
Molineaux, Private J., 31, 49
Mons, Battle of, 21, 67 121
Moorgate Cemetery, 72

Neuve Chapelle, 32, 67
Newhill, Wath upon Dearne, 97
Nicholson, Private, 111
Nixon, Corporal J., 105–6
North Lancaster Regiment, 121

Oldham, Private Frank B., 35

Page, John William, 56–7
Park Street, Rosehill, Rawmarsh, 59

Peasehill Street, Rawmarsh, 50
Percy Street, 17
Peter Street, Kimberworth, 99
Poilecourt, Prison of War Camp, 123–4
Porter, Private James William, 129–31
Porter, Private, Walter, 131–2
Porter, Private, William Henry, 131
Potter Hill, Greasbrough, 82
Preston, Rifleman, Robert, 35
Psalters Lane, Holmes, 58, 129

Rawmarsh Road, 100
Richardson, Captain Donald Hickling, 95–6
Richmond Barracks, Dublin, 36
Red Cross, 21, 97, 104, 122
Red Lion Hotel, 78–81
Roebuck, Signaller M., 116–17
Rose, Lieutenant General Charles, 102
Rotherham Heavy Battery, 127
Rotherham Howitzer Brigade, 85–7, 127
Rotherham Main Colliery, 58, 69, 124
Royal Army Medical Corps, 97–101
Royal Engineers, 52–3, 56, 58
Royal Flying Corps, 91–2, 127
Royal Munster Fusiliers, 127
Royal Naval Division, 75
Royal Pioneer Corps, 125
Ryalls, Nurse, 97-9
Rylett, Lance Corporal, 42

Sandbeck Park, 19
Sanderson, Private Arthur, 99–100
Scholes, Private Alfred, 100
Schonhut, Alderman Frederick, 71

Schonhut, Frederick Charles, 71–2, 78–9
School Street, 30
Seaton, Private J.R., 83–5
Shakespeare Road, 91
Smith, Lady Mabel, 103
Somme, Battle of, 32–3
St Ann's Road, 90
St George's Hall, 17, 22
St John's Ambulance Brigade, 97
St Stephen's Church, 90
Sugden, Private Brian, 121–2

Territorial Army, 108
Thiepval Wood, 34
Thomson, Second Lieutenant Ronald, 52
Thorpe Hesley, 19
Trotter, Major General Sir J.K., 86, 113
Twigg, Private Richard, 58–9

Victoria Street, Maltby, 53

Wagelein, Karl, 78
Ward, Corporal J.A., 29–30
Warren, Francis Percy, 55–6
Weatherhogg, Mr E., 17, 22, 24, 90, 106–9, 111–12
West Riding Infantry, 17, 127
West Yorkshire Regiment, 127
Wharf Road, Tinsley, 25
White, Private T.C., 125–6
Wilfred Street, 58
William Street, Wellgate, 108
Winder, Private H.A., 35
Wittenburg Camp, 21
Women's Forage Corps, 83
Woodward, Private Frank, 121
Wortley Road, 17, 116
Wright, Private J., 69

YMCA, 24
York and Lancaster Regiment,
  17–18, 30–1, 34–5, 46, 49, 50–1,
  59, 75, 92, 94, 127, 131
Ypres, 30–1, 47, 85